Fruitcake Hill

A History and Memoir of Life on the Hill in a Family of 15

Gerald J. Kuecher, Ph.D.

CCB Publishing
British Columbia, Canada

Fruitcake Hill: A History and Memoir of Life on the Hill in a Family of 15

Copyright ©2008 by Gerald J. Kuecher, Ph.D.
ISBN-13 978-0-9809995-0-1
First Edition, 2nd printing

Library and Archives Canada Cataloguing in Publication

Kuecher, Gerald J., 1951-
Fruitcake Hill: A history and memoir of life on the hill in a family of 15 / written by Gerald J. Kuecher.
ISBN 978-0-9809995-0-1
Also available in electronic format.
1. Kuecher, Gerald J., 1951-. 2. Kuecher family. 3. Irish Americans--Illinois--Chicago--Biography. 4. Chicago (Ill.)--Biography.
I. Title.
F548.54.K83A3 2008   977.3'11043092   C2008-902998-4

Cover image by artist James Schloss: Painting of the farmhouse on the hill, Palos Hills, Illinois

The recollections presented in this document are largely those of the author. The author apologizes in advance if misrepresentations, inaccuracies, or omissions are encountered or perceived. Sibling names were not directly cited in this manuscript to protect their identities.
Genealogical information presented herein is the product of a multi-year search.

Publisher: CCB Publishing
              British Columbia, Canada
              www.ccbpublishing.com

This book is dedicated
to my parents, Babe and Bob Kuecher,
and the hilltop property they so dearly loved.

Fruitcake Hill

Acknowledgments

The author wishes to recognize the critical editing of this document by siblings Edweird (Ed), Molock (Carolyn), Bob Sr., Babe, Tassy (Mary Kathleen), and Belle (Julie). Mamie (Babe's sister) also contributed greatly, together with brothers-in-law Steve (now deceased) and Jim. I appreciate these and other contributions that made this a better and more positive document. In addition, I wish to thank Babe's gifted son, Liza (Bob Jr.), for his poetic contribution to page 4 in Chapter 1. I also wish to thank Chicago area novelist Caryn Lazar Amster, who inspired me to write through her novel entitled *Wee Folks*.

Personal and heartfelt thanks go to my wife, Jean, who supported me in this effort and put up with piles of papers for months on the dining room table. And heartfelt thanks are also extended to Tassy, Belle, Jean, and my daughter Krisann who provided encouragement, reminding me always that these were my personal memoirs and as such, family consensus was not an issue.

Fruitcake Hill

Chapter One

A Farmhouse on a Hill

We lived on a hill. Historians and geologists called our hill Blackbird Island. It was one of a few islands some 15-20 miles southwest of Chicago that remained emergent following the most recent high water stage of Lake Chicago some 2,000-5,000 years ago. Other islands in the vicinity included Blue Island, Worth Island, Mount Forest Island, and Stony Island. These islands became local sources for construction sands and gravels in the 19th, 20th, and 21st Centuries.

The lowlands surrounding the swale-like hills were largely composed of peaty topsoils and peats that accumulated atop ubiquitous glacial tills. Occasionally the peaty combustibles ignited and a slow burn ensued. Peat fires weren't obvious to the casual observer. They largely burned below ground and for periods ranging between a few days and a few years. For those living nearby, the curse of these fires was the eternal smoky haze that hung over the landscape.

A log cabin home was built on one of these swale-like hills in 1853 by the Richard O'Connell family (all legal records indicate they preferred to be called Connell), Irish immigrants to America from County Cork, Ireland. The log cabin was abandoned in 1871 and a two-story, utilitarian farmhouse was built about a hundred yards west of the cabin site. Neighbors called our home

"The house on the hill." Family members affectionately called the hill and the human drama surrounding it "Fruitcake Hill."

Descendants of the Richard O'Connell family have continuously occupied this hilltop property since 1853 and the farmhouse, specifically, since it was built in 1871. These descendants were directly or indirectly affected by the Irish potato blight of 1848-1853, the American Civil War of 1860-64, the Great Chicago Fire of 1871, the Columbian Exposition of 1893, the Iroquois Theater Fire of 1903, the excursion boat Eastland disaster of 1915, the Great Depression of 1929-35, two great world wars, Korea, Vietnam, the Our Lady of Angels Fire of 1958, President Kennedy's assassination in 1963, and the Oak Lawn Tornado and Big Snow weather events of 1967. These Irish immigrants knew tragedy, but they were nonetheless brimming with optimism to build a life in this new world.

The O'Connells lived, became sick, and died in or very near the farmhouse. There were no hospitals. And the causes of their deaths seem tragic in light of the medical improvements to which we have become accustomed. Scarlet fever, tuberculosis, measles, diphtheria, and polio were the main killers and cripplers of children while peptic ulcers, tetanus, diabetes, heart disease, lung disease, pneumonia, alcoholism, and work-related injuries claimed the majority of adult lives.

There is little doubt the O'Connells of 1871 and the residents of the farmhouse today would find each other considerably alien were they to somehow meet. And the photograph that follows clearly supports that contention.

Portrait of Margaret and Richard O'Connell, circa 1865.

Our Irish ancestors took up grain farming in an area southwest of Chicago that would become known as Palos. A poetic reflection on our Irish farming roots, written by one of the O'Connell descendants follows:

> *They were Irish farmers as we all know*
> *I can picture them now using a hoe*
> *Clearing the land, getting stuck in the mud*
> *Yearning for Ireland and the taste of a spud*

To their credit the O'Connells elected to give up on farming potatoes in America. Back in Ireland, potatoes brought their family a great hardship. So they tried their luck raising corn and oats. This was a gamble, in itself, because they knew very little about anything except potatoes. But they started with a new slate and made the best of it. And for that, one must admire them.

The 1871 farmhouse was a two story structure typical of homes on the plains in those days. It was painted white and had a very steep roof covered initially with cedar shakes and later with greenish asphalt-based shingles. It had a dank stone basement with steep stairs to the first floor, radiator heat, a bathroom and a dining room with a big west-facing bay window, and three bedrooms upstairs. A garage that was little more than a *lean-to* and a screened porch were added by the time of the 1885 photo. The garage led variously up a half-flight to the kitchen, up a full flight to a storage attic, and on the ground level to a wash basin room complete with a wringer washer.

The family room and dining room lay respectively between the porch (added to farmhouse around 1880) and the kitchen on the ground floor. The farmhouse had an 80 foot well for drinking water, a septic tank beneath the back yard and a drain trap in the front yard.

The farmhouse was oriented not on today's x-y coordinate system, but rather about 25 degrees skewed. This made reference to what became known as the East Bedroom and the West Bedroom a bit of a stretch. And before WW2, a chicken coop and granary was located at the hill's break in slope, about 40 yards to the east.

The farmhouse on the hill (photo circa 1885).

The old banister hand rail that graced the stairwell joining the family room to the upstairs bedrooms deserves some notice. It had a simple but elegant style and stood up to decades of kids sliding down it solo and down the adjacent stairs in baby baskets. Children typically watched movies after hours from atop the landing and scattered to the winds if an adult made a move to chase them. Several accidents occurred on or near the banister, including a pencil stuck in a hand, numerous falls, and a near-tragic shooting when our father mistook one of the children coming in late for an intruder.

5

The farmhouse was drafty because little to no insulation was built into the walls. And getting dressed on school mornings when the temperatures fell to zero and below zero required a spot on prized real estate, i.e., above radiator ducts and in front of the open oven. Getting a spot in these few square feet often meant the difference between a pleasant morning and a bad one.

The farmhouse contained a number of treasure drawers. Old drawers became rich hunting grounds largely because nobody took time to sort them. One might encounter old Indian head pennies, buffalo nickels, mercury dimes, silver dollars, old switches, shotgun shells, and other assorted paraphernalia. And loose floorboards were occasionally encountered, beneath which our ancestors may have stored their savings.

A brick addition was added to the old farmhouse between 1965 and 1966 because there simply was no room to maneuver. The new addition included three bedrooms, a large family room, two additional bathrooms and a full-sized basement. That was the good news. The bad news involved the bricklayer contracted to build it. He was a tireless grouch with a nasty mouth. "Get outta that sand pile!" he would roar. And the kids would scurry for cover.

A grove of spectacular oak trees could be seen through the dining room's bay windows, their black, deeply furrowed trunks topped by lime green canopies that changed in rhythm with the wind. Squirrel, deer, fox, and coyote frequented this verdant landscape, especially in the early morning and early evening sun. And because acorns were the fundamental food supply for the characters in this daily play, the dining room became affectionately known as *The Acorn Room*, and it was decorated accordingly.

The farmhouse on the hill (white, wooden structure) exhibiting the west-facing bay window and the new addition (brick structure) finished in 1966. Photo circa 1995.

Perhaps the most inconvenient aspect of the old farmhouse was its single bathroom. One could imagine the scene when two or three children may be in queue and patience wore thin when the one in the bathroom did not share the same sense of emergency as those in waiting.

Humans were not the only animals to take residence in the farmhouse. At one time, a family of 11 raccoons lived in the attic. They were trapped and taken far away (at least that was the story the adults told the kids). Mice also took occasional residence because over 135 years of continuous meals were delivered to those that lived there. Trapping the mice earned the children a bounty but it was always awkward explaining the snap of these traps to guests invited for dinner.

Changes happened slowly on our hill but the march of progress was a determined foe. By the year 1862, the O'Connells owned 240 acres of farmland in the Palos area; perhaps more later. But they sold these holdings over the years to Warren's sod nursery and by the time World War 2 ended, only 3.6 acres remained. This remains the property of the family today while all surrounding properties belong to Moraine Valley Community College.

The taxes on the property were only about 100 dollars per year back in 1950. But today, the hill and all its history is going the way of all open properties in land-hungry suburbia, i.e., covered by the stuff of cities. And life in the vicinity of our property slowly changed. First there was one house, then another and another. Then a high school was built. And before we knew it, the village had become a city (1958), the city approved an ordinance against discharging firearms (1970), and our rural hunting paradise was gone forever.

This story focuses on the experiences of Babe and Bob Kuecher's family on this farm property. These stories may be difficult to appreciate in their current cultural context. But this was the case in the southwestern suburbs of Chicago in the 1950's and 1960's, where townships more appropriately described the city fringe than towns, and suburbia in its modern sense had not yet arrived.

Chapter Two

Babe

Kathleen Virginia Doyle was born in 1924 in the City of Chicago. The younger of two children, Kathleen was born to an Irish family of considerable pedigree. Her great grandfather, Peter Doyle, emigrated from County Wexford, Ireland in 1848. Peter Doyle's youngest son, Austin Doyle, was born in Chicago in 1849 and served as Police Chief for the City of Chicago 1882-1890. Austin Doyle died in 1924 and at the time was one of the oldest native Chicagoans. Other Doyles were variously successful as business men, artists, priests, teachers, and educational administrators. The Doyles lived in a number of locations in the city and their survival skills focused on Irish connections and formal educations.

Kathleen's first year could be characterized as a city kid. Her family lived at 7310 South Princeton on the city's south side. But things changed forever when Babe's father, Robert Emmett Doyle (one of four sons born to Austin Doyle and Pauline Weishaar) died of a perforated ulcer in 1925.

Robert Emmett Doyle (Babe's father) in photo circa 1925

This forced her mother to work a teaching job at Hamline School in the City of Chicago and relinquish Kathleen's care to her maternal

grandmother, Julia O'Connell, in the country farmhouse. It was Julia who first called her Babe and the name stuck through the years. Babe and Julia became very close and Julia's personality largely formed Babe's. Babe developed a calm nature and learned to deal with problems as they presented themselves. Moreover Babe learned to trust that she would survive despite the chaos of any moment. This was the strength she would call on later in life to raise her own children.

Nana, Babe's mother, in photo circa mid-1930's.

Julia and Patrick
O'Connell;
photo circa 1880

The death of her father resulted in the separation of Babe from her older sister, Mary. When they did get together on weekends, it became apparent that Babe's farm life and Mary's city life were fundamentally different. Babe wanted to run and play while her sister wanted to sit and read. It was a classic case of country mouse and city mouse.

Babe sported blonde to light brown wavy hair and a fair skinned complexion, a combination that typified the Irish. She burned easily in the sun and her face flushed red when overheated. As an adult she would attain a height of 5 foot 7 inches and walked with a bit of a forward stoop. Babe was everyone's friend and had a powerful presence.

December 27, 1927 was a landmark event in Babe's life. She was only 3.5 years old at the time and the weather outside was very cold. The adults were outside slaughtering and dressing turkeys to be given as Christmas gifts and Babe was left alone. And in a moment of mischief, she accidentally ignited a broom in the oven. She then tried to extinguish it by beating it against a pile of papers left to start the oven. And when that didn't work, she beat the broom against the curtains, greatly accelerating the conflagration. Babe knew she was in trouble so she gathered some bread, butter, and sugar and hid in the pantry, eating it in consolation.

Julia found Babe in the pantry and asked her to follow her quickly upstairs to retrieve the family money she hid under a loose floorboard. Julia found the money and her purse but dropped her purse on the way down the stairs. Julia fumbled in the smoke looking for it and out of the haze a neighbor, Ed Lucas, found Julia, Babe, and the purse and escorted/carried them safely outside.

The farmhouse erupted in flames but was spared a total loss due to quick work by the men and the fortune that heavy rains had recently filled a nearby gravel pit. Considering the grip the fire had on the house and the car garage, it is a wonder it was saved. Scorched boards can be seen today in the attic. But surprisingly, no adult criticized Babe's behavior that day. It was considered an accident and that was the end of the matter. That is a tribute to the patience of the O'Connell family, especially to Julia. Babe admits suffering from nightmares about the fire and her role in it into her 60's. And when Babe inherited the damaged building later in her life she said on more than one occasion it would have been better had the farmhouse just burned to the ground.

Photo of the farmhouse and car garage circa 1928 that clearly exhibits the roof area repaired after the 1927 fire.

Babe was schooled in the old Victorian way. She attended the prestigious Academy of Our Lady (later called Longwood Academy) on Chicago's south side and learned the fine arts of piano, violin, chorale, charm, tap dancing, and manners, as well as the basic core curriculum of English, mathematics, history, and geography. She was a lady of refinement when she finished at the Academy. But her life had a distinct duality. While she was refined in her schooling and manners, she was still a farm child at heart and remembers how

Guinea hens would chase her around the yard and how mink would gain access to the chicken coop and kill the lot.

Babe took up golf as a youngster and exhibited some talent. She was selected from a competition at age 9 and awarded pass to a clinic teaching her the game. It gave her the opportunity to play with her mother, who picked up the game at the request of doctors suggesting it would be good for breaking up her abdominal adhesions.

Babe met her husband to-be, Bob, in 1939 when Bob came to the farmhouse to date her sister, Mary. Babe and Bob, however, discovered they were the better pair. They were married in 1943 when Babe was 18 and Bob was 23. Babe's mother, Nana, was not thrilled that Babe was marrying before she had learned a profession. But they married nonetheless. There is an amusing report that when Bob asked Nana for the hand of her daughter, Nana was sufficiently confused (knowing he had dated both girls) and asked "Which one?"

Babe and Bob home from the hospital with their first child, November 1943.

German men and Irish women were common marriages in the Palos area. They complemented each other well. German men liked to work and Irish women liked to raise children, and together they had a herd before they knew it.

When Bob returned from the European theatre of WW2, Babe's mother signed over what remained of the farm (3.6 acres) to Bob and Babe while Babe's sister, Mamie, moved to Joliet, Illinois to raise her family and continue her teaching career.

Babe was purebred Irish and ultimately had thirteen children with Bob. Her children exhibited the mix of Celtic and Viking bloodlines as some were dark haired while others were strawberry blondes and redheads. And all save three had light complexions and many of these had a crop of freckles.

Babe contributed a number of genetic trademarks to her offspring, including male pattern baldness, light eyebrows, double-jointed thumbs, flexible fingers, and skin so fair it was prone to sunburns and keratoses.

Thirteen children, anyone would agree, was a heavy load and it affected Babe's most basic decisions, like naming her children. Babe had one daughter who believed her formal name was Kathleen Mary and found out late in life her registered name was Mary Claire. Babe also had a son who believed his name was Lawrence Thomas, but Babe had actually named him Craig Michael. Likewise, she had a son who thought his formal name was William Claire but discovered it was Claire William upon filing for a marriage license. Babe was overwhelmed with demands made on her in an operation of this scale and apparently ran out of names. She used Claire as a default until she got home and then asked the family what they thought. Each time, the family reacted like it encountered a leper. "No way!" the kids would complain and proceed to choose a different name. The problem was nobody ever fixed the official records.

One may wonder how thirteen children could sleep in a three bedroom home if one of the bedrooms was the parents' room. Mercifully, there was a sort of revolving door regarding occupancy in each of the children's bedrooms. As older brothers left for the armed forces, younger ones replaced them. It was not uncommon, in those days, for four or more children to share each bedroom in two sets of bunk beds, with spillover into the parents' room. Under those conditions, perhaps the biggest miracle was that Babe and Bob ever had time alone to produce thirteen children.

Neighbors and friends gasped when we discussed how Babe coped with thirteen children. To this day I am unsure whether their gasps were attributed to pity, admiration, or both. But Babe gave it all away, seldom purchasing anything new for herself. She did have a particular penchant for shoes, however. Bob would complain she was the Imelda Marcos of Palos as she had some 20 pairs, many stored in their original boxes. Babe used a few of these shoe boxes to hide cash, but quickly forgot in which box the money was stored. This didn't bother Babe; however, as she thought this was a good savings technique for the hereafter. She claimed she would need the shoes for walking the heavenly streets and would need the cash in case she finds a Marshall Fields store.

Our mother was responsible for the task of feeding 13 children and 2 adults. It wasn't bad enough that my mother was required to feed her fifteen; she was also called on to feed everyone's friends. One memorable Easter Sunday our Pakistani friend, Khalid, called and asked if he could come over for dinner. He said he would like to bring along his friends as well, and in Babe's gracious hospitality, she encouraged him. A few hours later, Khalid and his five friends arrived for Babe's Easter dinner. When they saw the meat-of-choice was ham, they expressed their Muslim displeasure. "Well then, what would you like?" Babe asked. "We all like steaks" the Pakistani contingent responded. And Babe obliged them with steaks. Babe had a servant's heart.

Babe would shop at the local Royal Blue food store in Palos Heights. Her *modus operandi* was to shop with several of her children in tow. When finished, she and the children typically would push 4 or more full carts toward the checkout line. The store manager, witnessing this scene would announce "Attention! Attention! All baggers to the front!" This was intended, of course, to alert store personnel, but for all practical purposes, it told others in the store "Stop what you are doing and notice this family!" Growing up in our family was a constant spectacle. And the military-scale efforts to feed the lot usually relied more on simple repetition than culinary sophistication.

Cooking with Babe was a trip. Babe used recipes and took advice from Grandma and the older girls. But somehow, the kids thought they needed to keep a watchful eye on her. On one particular Thanksgiving morning, Babe put a very large turkey, complete with its bread crumb and celery stuffing into a double broiler at about 8:00 AM. After a few hours, she opened the oven door, lifted the upper broiler pan and through the steam the one of the boys noticed the bird was snow white and sighed, "Look Mom, you boiled it!"

Babe sheltered Bob from most of the bad news of the family, including the money situation. In fact Bob was unaware of his total financial outlays until he woke early one morning and saw Babe handing out money to every child leaving for the school's weekly hot dog day. It was staggering and Bob was a whole lot better off not knowing. Thank God Bob made enough money to feed us.

The bad news for Babe in living on the hill was the scourge of dust. When farmers plowed and when they harvested, dust would waft over the terrain and settle on our house. A sod company owned the area immediately surrounding our home and needless to say they contributed their fair share. But Babe could not keep up. It was like forever being in a construction site. To complicate matters, we paved our own road with crushed dolomite. This in time became (you guessed it) dust. "Close the doors, the trucks are coming!" was Babe's desperate cry from the hill. Exacerbating the problem, Babe's youngest child, Edweird peddled his tricycle down the road dragging a rake. We would ask, "What are you doing, Ed?" "Makin' moke," he would respond. As if Babe needed more!

The most embarrassing thing about being in a big family was being late for virtually every engagement. We were late for school, late for church, late for parties, late for graduation, late for everything. My mother did the best she could, God bless her, but the job was too great. We may have been within minutes of leaving *en masse* when Babe would notice one child with dirt under the fingernails and that would derail the train. "Get in the bathroom and scrub your nails!" she would say. We exhausted the patience of the school district, the church, the Cub Scouts, the Little League, the school bus drivers, and every agency with which we had dealings. To make matters worse, we typically pulled in late with a very noisy diesel car announcing our tardiness, even to the deaf. No sneaking in un-noticed with our family! We children, of course wanted desperately to blend in like everyone else but that was just impossible. One day Babe may force the bus off the road and the next day she may run into a snow bank and we were forced to run to the bus. These mad rushes occasionally resulted in fingers being smashed in car doors, and such an accident typically set the departure back a half-hour or more. So embarrassed were the children by our repeated walks of shame into waiting buses, classrooms-in-progress, and Catholic masses near their end that some of us wished we could just fade into the wallpaper and go unnoticed. And if the diesel car noise didn't shake passers-by with its decibel level, they would surely notice that the car smelled like a chicken fry as it passed them, as Bob was experimenting with bio-diesel way back in the early 1960's. Heck, Babe was even late going to the hospital to deliver her babies and was forced, on one occasion, to push the baby back so she didn't deliver in the car.

A dream one of the children experienced as a teenager

summarized our collective frustration. In it, the dreamer dreamed he was the back of a short school bus. The bus was driving by the farmhouse. Normally the bus would be obligated to wait for our family. On this occasion, however, the dreamer sensed an option. Seeing one of his brothers coming down the hill struggling to put his tie on, his mother flagging the bus down, and his sister running and spilling her lunchbox contents, the bus driver looked into his rectangular rear view mirror and asked, "Does anybody know these people?" The dreamer made eye contact with the driver and said "No!" and the bus passed them by. One does not need to be the Biblical Joseph to interpret this dream.

A lesser but still memorable embarrassment for the children involved our Catholic school uniforms. As the word uniform implies, there was little room for individuality. That worked well with most families. But Babe, on occasion, did not have the regulation blue plaid shirts and the skirts cleaned and pressed. So at the last minute, just before the bus arrived, Babe may say, "Here, put this on, nobody will notice." "Are you joking? There must be some mistake! You want me to wear this pink shirt on class picture day?" The embarrassment was sometimes too much to bear.

Babe had a lot on her plate, however, and between washing the clothes, picking up kids, and preparing meals she occasionally got flustered. Such was the case when she was arrested by store security for inadvertently putting something in a bag. Store authorities recognized she was just confused and advised her to go home and get some rest.

Similarly, a traffic policeman once stopped Babe and asked, "Maam, may I see your driver's license?" After several minutes of searching through her purse, the policeman then asked, "Maam may I see your vehicle registration?" Babe continued to search through coupons and other materials muttering, "Oh they must be here somewhere!" In utter desperation, the officer resigned and told Babe to be more careful next time. She's much the same today. Just ask her to find something in her purse!

Babe tried many times to do the wash in Palos but complained the well water was of poor quality and the clothes were being ruined by it. Instead she bundled the wash, packed it into her car and drove to her mother's home in Beverly, where she had high quality water from Lake Michigan. Perhaps she also needed to get away for a few hours and be with her mother. Then there was the safety issue. Back then the washers had dangerous wringer devices that pulled wet clothes through them. If children's fingers just happened to get caught in those wringers, Babe would be there to strike the release.

Babe tried to set up a system whereby the older children, raised entirely by her, assisted in the care of the younger ones. But the job was too great and she asked for outside help from an African American lady named Leola, who lived about 20 minutes away in Robbins, Illinois. Leola dug Babe out of the farmhouse's accumulated trash and grime once a week. All of us can remember the fried potato and onions she would prepare while listening to White Sox games. But an even more amazing event occurred one day as Leola was waiting in our car to be driven home. She was in the passenger seat in her coat and hat. Then the car, apparently left in neutral, began to roll backward down the hill's driveway. Leola had no clue how to stop this eventuality and just froze, slack-jawed and white eyed. The car ran into a tree half-way down the hill and Leola stepped out. Never again would she sit in the vehicle unattended.

Babe was quick to remind the children that our most important duty before we left the home for an evening was to change our underwear. She said we had to have clean underwear should we end up in a hospital. This is one reason why we all ended up slightly screwy. We were led to believe someone would inspect our under-wear should we leave home. It was a lot easier just staying home.

Bob occasionally sent Babe on errands for parts to keep the shop going. She reflects that these driving trips brought her some sanity. She could drive away from the hubbub of the hill and leave it all behind.

Our mother had a very Catholic outlook and one of her hang-ups involved children being exposed to sex before their time. To say the 's' word or refer to a 's'- related issue in our home was a cause for blush. We felt Babe's embarrassment and tried to shelter her from it. A daily issue she dealt with, for lack of room in the family car, involved girls sitting on the laps of the boys. This was a no-no in inner Catholic circles. Hard core Catholics, we were told, carried phone books for the laps of the boys. No one remembers how Babe dealt with these issues. But the expediency of everyday life, in all its imperfections, no doubt superseded such lofty guidelines.

Babe's uneasiness with sexual issues came to a zenith one particularly cold morning. Looking out the frosty kitchen window, the children observed a very unusual phenomenon. Our very large and thick Shetland pony, Bubbles, was enveloped in a dense fog. On closer inspection we noticed the steam was radiating from his highly enlarged male member. Babe, noticing a number of faces staring out the window snapped, "Get away from those windows!" We'd walk away from such a shameful experience citing "mea culpa, mea culpa, mea maxima culpa," convenient Latin phrases we learned as altar boys to deal with our shame. If that didn't come to mind we could repeat the prayer "Lord I am not worthy" about a gazillion times."

Babe was an advocate of a number of Catholic practices such as burying St. Joseph statues upside down in lawns to sell homes and sprinkling holy water over her lottery tickets. These actions gave her a distinct advantage over non-believers, or so she thought. And she prayed to a number of saints of whom the children never heard. In fact, if Babe cared to share her thoughts about a relative that had passed on, she would gather her box of funeral holy cards and speak to you about them. Photos were not required!

But if God loves the person who gives their all in this life, then He surely has reserved a place for Babe. We distinctly remember the look on Babe's face when she heard the account of the witnesses to the miracle at Knock, Ireland. When asked how the witnesses knew for certain the identity of Jesus, Mary, Mary Magdaline, and Joseph in this apparition, they replied in typical Irish logic, "Because they looked exactly like the statues out front!" Babe knew logically this popped the balloon on the miracle but if it's good enough for the Pope, it was good enough for her.

Babe's favorite saying, "Be it ever thus," was a paraphrase from a prayer or Biblical teaching, perhaps "Is now and ever shall be." Paraphrasing verses was a Catholic trait, i.e., our efforts to quote prayers or the Bible did not have to be, nor were they expected to be verbatim. That was the job of the priests. We, after all, were the ignorant flock.

Babe accumulated a pill warehouse over the years that would rival Squibb. These pills represented the combined leftovers from hundreds of childhood ailments. Many of these pills were expired, and their bottles, with written names and dosages were often times long gone. But Babe kept them all and administered the drugs to her children and passers-by with a methodology that would make her Irish heritage proud. "Here, take one of these blue pills. You're not looking well," Babe would say. "What is it?" asked the victim. "Oh, it's probably an antibiotic," Babe would say. God forbid if you exhibited more complex symptoms. The color and size variations would then increase exponentially. Babe may say, "You need to try the small pink pills" or "If that doesn't work try the large purple ones." The FDA would have arrested Babe had they known, but the amazing thing is she was usually right in her diagnoses, prescriptions, and dosages.

Babe suffered silently on a number of levels. She suffered emotionally with her family and she suffered physically as well. She developed bursitis in her shoulder and had to get a number of painful cortisone injections. But because Bob was busy in the shop, Babe was typically unaccompanied by any other adult in her visits to the doctor and had to drive a stick shift home. We remember her crying upon returning home.

We all knew Babe was good, but she elevated herself to legendary one night when the grandchildren decided to camp in our back yard. Granted, we did not have a typical back yard, as over 160 acres buffered us from neighbors, and a pack of coyotes were known to run in our surroundings. So the adults had a case of anxiety when the children, generally less than 10 years old, decided they wanted an un-chaperoned night in the tent. By 10:00 PM, we began to hear the yelps. First they were far away, and then they grew closer. By midnight, the pack had descended on our hill and the yelps were upon us. What if one of the little ones had to get up and go potty outside the tent? Could a grown coyote run off with a small child? We were just about to go outside and terminate this exercise when we heard a window slide open and Babe yelled, "Git! Git!" The coyotes, astoundingly, backed off and the rest of the night was smooth sailing! Babe had become a rock star.

Babe's mother, Nana, visited the farm house occasionally. We could easily spot her big black and white Pontiac as it crossed the bridge on 111th Street and turned down our long and dusty road. Nana was citified from her many years in Beverly and was distant from the reality of the hill. In addition, she really did not understand boys and how boys played. She never had one. So on one visit she gathered all the boys' play pistols, rifles, swords, and other weapons of mass destruction and they were never seen again. She said she threw them into the canal. Among these toys Nana threw away the boys new set of Fanner 50s. It was hard to forgive her for that. Nana died in a Joliet hospital in 1977 from complications following hip replacement surgery.

Babe's record-keeping left a lot to be desired. She would save virtually every receipt and note on the dining room table, but seldom did she organize by category. Instead, she pulled out boxes of receipts near tax deadline and tried to sort them post-facto. Realizing she was hopelessly behind and that she would not be able to submit by tax deadline, she annually took the easy route and asked for an extension. And because Babe was so overwhelmed with other affairs, she soon racked up eight years in arrears before her children worked to bail her out.

Perhaps Babe is most infamous in family circles regarding her penchant for shopping. Bob used to say Babe's favorite words were "Charge it!" and he claims Babe personally funded the stock value at Marshall Fields Store in Chicago. Let there be no mistake, Babe did spend some money, especially in shopping for 15 people. But, in her defense, she was not a wasteful shopper and it was common that she would be gone the better part of a day when she did go shopping.

When Babe stopped to shop at the Evergreen Park Mall she typically had a few of her children in tow. Boys however had little patience for shopping if the shopping did not involve them. In these cases, Babe showed some real creativity. She parked the boys at the monkey cage in Lyttons Department Store. The monkeys and the boys had a way of entertaining each other and time passed. Babe would return an hour later and there they were, sharing antics. Men are basically the same today. They could watch monkeys, a baseball game, or people passing for hours. Shopping malls caught on to this and placed chairs on which men could sit. Kudos to common sense.

Despite the bumpkin-like exterior of our life on the hill, Babe did her best to expose us to cultural events. She would purchase tickets for us to the Nutcracker, Snow White, Ice Capades, the Shriners Circus, the Field Museum, the Science and Industry Museum, Drury Lane Theatre, McCormick Place, and other outings in the City of Chicago. And we would all attend in our finest outfits. Babe cared about our total education, including shopping at "the world's finest department store, Marshall Fields."

Lotto tickets that Babe purchased weekly provided her with the dream that a lucky break would some day be hers. And she would dance about in a mini-jig thinking how she would transform her own and her children's lives if she were somehow blessed with such fortune. This same philosophy that fortune was around the next corner prompted Babe to invest (perhaps unwisely) in family businesses. Her spirit was indelibly stamped Celtic.

Babe continued to drive into her mid-eighties largely because mobility was fundamental to her mental health. But Babe was too blind to see and too proud to quit her driving. Bob claimed that Babe owned a set of glasses but didn't like to wear them. And she positioned them on her lap to quickly place them on her head should a patrolman stop her. A lot of good that did, eh!

Babe never seemed to cry openly at wakes or funerals. The kids reasoned she had seen a lot of death in her days, but there was more to it. We were getting a peek into her Irish psyche. The Irish, after all, invented the wake, presumably to keep vigil for evil spirits but in actuality a thinly-veiled occasion to drink. Babe remembered with great fondness the Mary Tully funeral in which two of her boys had a field day running amok. To Babe's Irish eyes, joy should be a part of the Irish funeral experience. And she said on more than one occasion that Mary would have wanted it to be that way. Life was hard for the Irish and death, an occasional drink, and unmitigated joy was its release. Don't ask too many questions as the answer may be too much to bear. In fact, Sigmund Freud once remarked "The Irish are one race of people for which psychoanalysis is of no use whatsoever."

When the boys were of high school and college age, Babe developed a method to check if they were drinking. She would lock the door so she would be awakened on their return, and on opening the door she would say, "Come here and kiss your mother." Of course, that was the set-up for her to smell your breath, and she would exclaim, "You've been drinking, haven't you?" Oh, Babe was clever!

Babe's sister, Mamie, was known as *the Leprechuan of Joliet*. Each and every year she sent St. Patrick's Day cards to all her children, her grandchildren, and the cousins. We looked forward to opening these cards because its arrival pronounced that Irish magic was alive and well for those who believed. She also started a tradition that her family would get together each St. Patrick's Day and give thanks they were born Irish. At these get-togethers, the family enjoyed Irish soda bread, corned beef, cabbage, and generous quantities of Guinness. We may even sit down together to watch *The Quiet Man*. Everyone's favorite part occurred when the horse pulling Mickeleen Flynn's courting surrey stopped abruptly outside the tavern. "Oh you've got more sense than us all" Mickeleen exclaimed.

Mamie was an elementary school teacher for 32 years. Her first assignment commenced in 1948 at a red country schoolhouse off 104th Avenue in Palos Township where she had 11 students in five different grade levels. This historic schoolhouse was later moved to its present site in a nature preserve, a move of about two hundred meters. She later accepted a teaching assignment in the Joliet area. We all remember Mamie's recollections of her student-from-hell, Roger. This kid was a living nightmare. And unless a miracle saved him, he is probably serving time today in a corrections facility.

Mamie expressed a keen interest that her children and grandchildren visit their Irish homeland and gain an appreciation of their ancestors and their trek. Consistent with that desire, Mamie traveled to Ireland in 2003 with her daughters Mellen, Dorothy, nephew Tiger, and his wife, Jean. All attending were so privileged to have shared that time with her. It was, in retrospect, our last opportunity to be with her in her beloved Emerald Isle.

Mamie contracted cancer in her early 80's. A few years and a surgery later, Mamie was advised by her physician that she had perhaps two weeks to live. This news didn't shock Mamie. In fact, she mentioned she had waited 54 years to be re-united with her husband and she was looking forward seeing him again. This was the Irish spirit we learned as youngsters, years before at the Mary Tully funeral. But Mamie went a step further. She paid for her own funeral so she would not burden her children and she paid for a luncheon following the internment. She even purchased a forest green casket that would make the Irish proud! And to top things off, she purchased Christmas gifts for her grandchildren that were delivered months after her death. This was Irish magic, a modern resurrection of sorts. To Mamie's Irish mind, wakes were meant for the living. This was a testament to her Catholic faith, i.e., she had total trust her loved ones were bound for heaven and there was nothing to whimper about.

Mamie (Babe's sister) in a photo a few months prior to her passing in 2006.

The astounding thing about Mary's desire to be re-united with her husband concerned the conditions between them as a couple in his final year. Letters written by Mary and returned to her by the Air Force following his death included pleas by Mary to send his paycheck home to support his five children. But he presumably had a gambling addiction and his monies were often spent as quickly as he received them. On his final day alive, he was reported to have left Mather Air Force Base near Sacramento, California, with 700 dollars in his pocket. He was later found murdered and floating in the Sacramento River.

Air Force pilot James Kenney, shortly before his death in California

Mary's husband never saw his youngest daughter because he failed to return home following the leave that left Mary pregnant the final time. This same daughter married 22 years hence and her husband, likewise, died prematurely. Like Mary's husband, he never laid eyes on his own daughter. Furthermore, the gambling addiction that doomed Mary's husband revealed itself in subsequent generations in both Babe's and Mary's families. We pray these patterns are now broken.

Babe, unlike her sister Mary, showed little interest in things or traditions Irish. But she was keenly interested in the living genealogy of her ancestors, i.e. the stories that made their lives more than a collection of birth, marriage, and death dates.

Chapter Three

Bob

Our father was nicknamed Bob although his real name was Francis Robert. Bob, of German and Czech Bohemian descent, was born in the year 1919 in the City of Chicago in the vicinity of St. Basil's Parish, 1850 W. Garfield Boulevard. He moved with his family to the Palos area the following year, where his family found employment as tavern keepers, rooming house operators, mechanics, and later in black dirt mining and sales. Bob remembers the Prohibition and how Mafia types would come to Palos and spend money. They would picnic at a lake property owned by Bob's grandfather, Frank Tampier (known today as Tampier Slough), and bring the finest steaks, fruits, and of course whiskey to celebrate with their families. Bob's family knew these people as friendly clients and they were astounded to hear that many of these folks were murdered within a few miles of their business.

Frank Tampier's passport indicated he emigrated from Austria although the family emigrated from modern day Czechoslovakia near the beer making town of Budejovice (original name for Budweiser). Austria, you see was quite a bit larger at the time of the first great war.

Frank Tampier worked for years with his son George in black dirt mining and Tampier Slough (now a Cook County Forest Preserve property) resulted from these dirt mining operations.

Frank was a real outdoorsman and he hunted and fished

whenever possible. He would shoot a bunch of pheasants or ducks and it was Grandma's job was to clean them. George also was a terrific trapper. On his lake property, thousands of muskrat hutches dotted the surface, like pepper on a plate. Back in the 1930's, the Chicago furriers offered $3.00 for each nicely skinned muskrat pelt. And George one year traded 1400 of these pelts for cash. Bob remembers he purchased a new car, a new wardrobe, a wardrobe for his wife, and various other things with the proceeds.

Bob said he never saw his grandfather make his own cup of coffee. His grandfather would sit and Grandma would bring him his coffee. Then she would add the sugar and cream and stir it with a spoon. He did not have to raise a finger in the house. He was the King!

Bob had a wonderful, hard-working mother and a pot-bellied father with whom he did not relate. His father, Frank Kuecher, worked in Lyons, Illinois as a night foreman at ElectroMotive Company while his mother was a stay at home Mom.

Bob had musical talent and learned to play the saxophone and the clarinet as a child. He seldom read sheet music and instead performed largely by ear and memory. Music was one vehicle through which Bob's father gave him respect and attention. His father often played along on a mouth organ while his mother, known to the kids as Grandma, sang. Grandma had great appreciation for music and learned all the operas by listening to a Saturday afternoon radio program *All about the Operas*, on Texaco Star Theatre. She would sing as she ironed the clothes and learned most of the operas by heart. Back then there was no TV and the people listened to radios.

Frank died of a heart attack in Palos when Bob was in his early 30's. Bob's Bohemian mother, however, lived many years thereafter and spent a good deal of her time cooking a number of wild animals and wild animal parts that one may consider soul food today. She cooked pig's feet, ox tails, beef tongue, chicken gizzards, beef liver, heart, and other parts as well as wild animals e.g., squirrels, raccoon, bear, rabbits, turtles, pheasant, ducks, and geese. If it were dead, Grandma would cook it. It was as simple as that. In fact, Grandma Kuecher's favorite part of birds was the triangular part that made it over the fence last (the tail). We said, "Oh, Grandma! How could you?" But Grandma kept on snacking as though she was privy to the greatest secret ever!

Bob never had much formal education because times were hard in the 1920's. His family needed his meager contributions because the family was in survival mode. So Bob finished 8th grade at Palos Elementary School and that was considered progress because his mother only finished the 6th grade. But neither Bob's nor his mother's education ended in elementary school.

Bob worked as a young teen by hauling water in milk cans to the canal workers in his modified Model T Ford. Later he worked 3 years as a brewer in Cincinnati with his uncle, Bill, and spent 14 years at Buda Diesel where he learned his life's craft, heavy equipment engine development. This is amusing because his German (possibly Ukrainian) surname meant coachman, as in a driver of a team of horses, or heavy equipment operator, i.e., what he does today.

Palos was a very different place in the 1930's and 1940's when Bob grew up. There were resources and land was available. Black dirt, sand and gravel, sod, construction, cement, and other industries sprung up in the Palos area. It appeared that anyone with vision, a hard work ethic, and some guts could make it. Such a market created its own lot of colorful individuals. Bob remembers quite clearly, for example, when a local gravel pit operator named Ed Dea purchased a brand new Buick Century convertible with his earnings and brought it home. After a few minutes of admiration, his son asked to go for a ride. Then he said, "But Daddy, we can't leave the pony home." So they put the pony in the back seat of this brand new vehicle and off to the bar they went. They returned home a few hours later with a damaged vehicle on day one of ownership.

Bob was drafted into the army in 1942 and headed off to the European theatre in 1944. The worst part of that assignment, Bob recalled, was crossing the big pond in a barely sea-worthy, troop carrier that held about 3,000 soldiers. Within a few miles of departure, Bob and hundreds of other young soldiers were so sick they pleaded for death to just end it! Luckily, however, Bob made a great friend, Steve, who cared for him in the nasty crossing, bringing him crackers and water

During the war, Bob volunteered to drive the Captain of the C-Company 35th Tank Battalion around in a jeep. He was officially trained to drive tanks. But Bob saw the writing on the wall: Allied tank survival was measured in days against the far superior German tanks. But in his capacity as jeep driver, Bob lived through the Battle of the Bulge and drove on with his division into Czechoslovakia. In the final days of the war, enemy soldiers surrendered *en masse* and on one occasion over a hundred German soldiers came out of the woods with their hands up to surrender to this solitary soldier in his jeep. They apparently realized the war was lost and just wanted to go home.

In those final days, Bob witnessed the surrender of a German aerial reconnaissance plane known as the *Fiesler Storch.* This plane was designed to fly above the battlefields and survey enemy troop movements. This particular plane landed in clear sight of Bob's division in Pisek, Czechoslovakia with the arms of the pilot flailing to signal his surrender. It was a brand new airplane, and the American Captain asked if there was anybody from his company that might know how to fly it. Bob was very mechanical and had a student pilot license. So in brash confidence he said he could. And after a few practice taxis down the prairie runway, he and the Captain departed and got a peek at the battlefield that only such a plane could see. Within an hour, however, they encountered friendly

Allied fire. So they quickly returned and had the plane painted with stars on the undercarriage. Bob and another soldier then flew this airplane over the Alps and down the Danube River to Regensberg, Germany where the remainder of the company had moved by truck. Today, Bob hangs an action photo of a Fiesler Storch in his bedroom as a remembrance of this exhilarating ride at war's end.

Bob came home from war unharmed while his friend Steve returned with metal plates in his head, the result of sticking his head out of his tank when the clearance at an underpass was not sufficient. Both Bob and Steve, however, considered themselves lucky and they spent time with each other perhaps every other Sunday in unending celebration that they survived. Steve and his wife, Helene, later became godparents to Bob and Babe's youngest son.

Bob was an imposing man, standing 6 feet 3 inches tall. He had long arms and gigantic hands that were permanently stained with grease no matter what efforts were put to cleaning them. He wore a work uniform in his garage, but unlike our school uniforms, a cleaning company regularly picked up his soiled clothes and returned them clean and folded. The name tag on his work shirt said *Bob* but we all called him *BO Bob* for olfactory reasons.

When Bob returned from WW2, he started an auto repair shop. This business became, in time, a diesel machine shop that converted gasoline powered trucks to diesel about 50-60 yards from the farmhouse. His original shop building was small, boxy in plan, and located approximately where the chicken coop lay in earlier days. Bob's original shop included a tall reference bookshelf and billing area, a drill press, a lathe, some block and tackle to lift engines, a hydraulic press, and a coal-fired furnace the children had to feed regularly in winter months. On the walls, discolored Polaroid photos were tacked adjacent to an ancient wind-up type army field phone in a ragged leather case. That phone, as we recall, was only good to call the house a short distance away, if you didn't get shocked first.

In time, however, Bob's business expanded and he built two large, adjoining cement block garages that were partially lit by glass block. We called these new garages the Middle Garage and the Big Garage. The activity level of Bob's garages was easy to assess by just walking through them.

Bob employed a nephew to help him in the shop. His nickname was Tarbender and he was a few years older than the oldest boys. Tarbender, sometimes called Black Bart because his beard came in so dark, considered it his duty to educate the boys in his considerable street knowledge. Conversations between the boys and Tarbender went something like this: "What honey did you go out with last night?" To which the boys might answer "Oh, I stayed in but had a good time." "That's what she said to me last night" Tarbender would respond and he'd laugh and laugh! Another favorite Tarbender opening line was, "Are you working hard or hardly working?" This level of conversation was about all you got out of him, although he would speak for hours of his fishing and hunting experiences.

Tarbender worked outside fixing heavy machinery and liked to drink cold soda pop. So during the summer months he would enlist the boys daily, and perhaps twice a day to walk to the tavern and pick up some assorted bottles of soda pop. Back then, the bottles were refundable. So as we nurtured Tarbender's obsession with soda pop, we were also stockpiling the spent bottles for a cash return, a symbiotic relationship. On the day of the bottle run, an older boy would typically push the wheel barrow while a younger boy pulled the red wagon. When these vehicles were filled from stops in the garage, bottles picked up in ditches enroute, and a stop by Granny Durack's house in the neighborhood, we could earn a profit between four and six dollars. That was big money for kids in the early 1960's.

Bob worked in his shop from 8:00 AM to 5:30 PM. He then came into the house for dinner, watched the 6:00 news, and returned to work in the shop between the hours of 7:00 and 10:00 PM. When he retired for the day, he enjoyed sardines in olive oil, limburger "stinky" cheese on crackers, a beer, and a cigarette while watching The Late Show. He also enjoyed a shot of Crown Royal or Seagrams whiskey at the end of the day and had a ritual whereupon drinking his portion bottoms-up, he would shake his head and sigh, "Oooh that's good booze!" in typical Gleason-esque fashion.

Bob believed in allowing his kids the freedom to taste beer or try a cigarette in the home. This he believed would encourage moderation in such choices later in life. That was a good and effective policy. One habit Bob had, however, was to extinguish his cigarette in the beer can. And on one memorable occasion, a middle child found a beer can aside Bob's Lazy-boy that had a bit remaining. So he lifted the can, drank the contents and got a mouthful of revolting cigarette sludge. That particular child never tried a cigarette again.

Bob, on occasion, cut the boys' hair. The boy selected for the haircut would sit in a small chair placed atop the kitchen table. This allowed Bob to get close to his subject. At this point, a towel was affixed around the neck and Bob started his electric shears. No special requests were allowed. These were generic *doos*, nothing special. Flat top and cue ball were the only style options. Tears were occasionally shed by the younger boys, largely because they didn't trust they would survive the ordeal without being nipped by the razor.

Bob had a .357 Magnum pistol that he liked to target shoot. So he built a backstop of 3/16" steel plate and practiced on Sunday afternoons with Babe's cousin, Claire (where have we heard that name?) and a few of his colleagues from the Illinois State Police. When the shooting was over, the kids would go through the sand below the stop and find the flattened lead pieces. Somehow this was amusing.

Because we had such a large family and had sizeable needs,

folks would stop by with various contributions. One older gent, Andy, would stop by on Saturday mornings with leftover donuts from his friend's bake shop. These were given in exchange for services Bob would render. We didn't mind these donuts were stale. They were sweet and that was good enough for us. And occasionally a box of clothes was dropped by. Babe may pitch a pair of coveralls to us and say, "Try these on." The boys would plead for mercy because some were obviously women's cuts with zippers up the side. That argument didn't make much hay with Babe who had no experience taking an emergency whiz when you are bound like a cocoon!

Babe and Bob made a slightly odd couple. Babe was the lady from finishing school while Bob was the boy that dropped out of school and a bit rough in his ways.

They maintained humor throughout their trials, however, and never considered divorce. Babe would sit with Bob and laugh at Red Skelton on television. One of Bob's favorite Skelton jokes went like this, "I married Mrs. Right. I just didn't know her first name was Always." And he showed humor in dealing with young ladies he did not know, although there was the issue of a slightly inflated machismo. For example he may, upon meeting a young lady, turn to those in attendance and say, "See, she's crazy about me." To which we all may respond, "You've got to be crazy to think she's crazy about you." Certainly someone was crazy here.

Bob came from a family of two children and his sister had three. So Babe's penchant for children was unprecedented in Bob's worldview. When they passed three, Bob and Babe were in uncharted waters. But post-war optimism was high and having children seemed like the right thing to do. Bob would trust Babe on this matter. His job was to support them with his income. But one must speculate what Bob must have thought when the tally passed five, then ten, and finally thirteen. Alexander the Great was reported to once having faced a similar dilemma when he was advised that his army had marched off the known map of the world. His officers offered advice that he should turn back. But Alexander was said to have replied, "Lesser armies would turn back." I think Bob was kind of like Alexander here.

Bob was king of the hill and did not feel comfortable venturing off of it. Visits to the barber, the doctor, or church were all he could handle. He liked to say he had never been to any of the grown kids' houses, so why start now. Most of the kids found this a weak excuse but Bob usually provided time when they visited him

Bob did enjoy his yearly fishing trip to Canada, however, and each year took a few of the kids along. But six days in a tent with this man was a trial. Specifically, we had no idea how he snored! It was not a cyclic, repetitive, healthy snore. No it was more staccato, building to a crescendo, and abruptly stopping, no more breathing (the man must have died), followed by a massive exhale type of snoring. Begin cycle again. Babe should have warned us. So by the second night we realized that if we were going to get any sleep we'd better get a head start on the old man and retire early.

On one memorable drive to Canada, one of the younger boys was sleeping in the rear seat on the passenger side when his older brother, a relatively inexperienced driver, was forced to apply the brakes. A full quart steel Stanley coffee thermos rolled off the rear window and fell on his head in a distinct clunk. Then we saw blood spurting. The car was stopped and Bob applied a towel to stop the bleeding. It was an ugly scene that required stitches at a nearby hospital.

The following morning, as we approached the outfitters access road in the Boundary Waters area on the Minnesota-Canadian border, Bob made the decision to forge ahead in floodwaters despite warnings by locals not to do so. At the time we had a brand new green Pontiac Le Mans and within minutes we realized this was not going to be easy. The boat behind us was floating to the left and right and the vehicle was in water so deep that it flooded through the doors. But we trudged ahead regardless and once we arrived at our outfitter on Crane Lake, we pulled the carpeting out of the car and aired it out for a week. Bob said his friend, Al, would take care of him at the lodge. But when Al approached our family at the breakfast table, and said, "Bob Krueger! How are you, Bob Krueger?" The kids found this amusing. We figured we were in trouble if his friend didn't even know his name.

Bob at one time had ideas of moving to Australia. He thought all his problems would disappear or something. And as children, we didn't know if we were staying or going.

Finally, Bob vacationed in Australia for about three weeks and got it out of his system. During this time, his mother, Grandma Kuecher, stayed with us, made meals and helped out. By the time they came back she was more than ready to release that burden back to Babe. A few years later Bob, Babe, and Mamie sojourned through the south and into Mexico. These trips broadened Bob's worldview from one centered on the hill to a more global perspective. Bob's dreams of escape to another land died a slow death, however, and we watched the sun set on those dreams.

Bob was a creative genius and took pride that he was a true mechanic and not a parts changer. He was engineer-designer-mechanic-machinist in one. He dreamed big dreams and accomplished big things. And he took time out of his own job to invent. The only thing that held Bob back from even greater heights was his inability to market his products or himself. Not many inventors are good at that, however. They prefer to be left alone. So Bob's many inventions, like the diesel powered Studebaker, the bio-diesel Gremlin vehicle that ran on Kentucky Fried Chicken grease, the power plant that freed him from buying Commonwealth Edison electricity, and the automated sod cutting and rolling machine could have been successfully marketed had Bob cared more about sales and marketing.

Bob was involved in the major crises of the family. One such crisis involved our horse, Red Satin. The horse was tall, perhaps 17 hands high and sorrel in color. One day while grazing, Red Satin managed to fall through the wooden well cover into the well sump pit. The pit consisted of concrete walls and a concrete floor. The walls were about 7 feet square, and the pit measured about 6 feet deep. On the pit floor stood an electrical pump motor mounted on a wooden skid. The horse was pinned in that tight confine, its neck and head out of the hole and its feet stepping all over the pump at the base of the pit. The horse produced numerous surges of energy (he was being shocked) in which he kicked the hell out of the pump, realized escape was futile, and each time settled down. In time, the horse's spirit began to fade and his eyes began to roll back in his head. But while the younger kids were variously crying or pacing nervously about, my father and my oldest brother tailored a chain and thick blankets into a sling-like apparatus and with the help of a cat tractor lifted the horse to safety. We knew all was well when the horse, unconscious of the great human effort expended to save him, ignored us and began eating his damned grass.

Bob, on the day following this ordeal, wrote a note excusing one of the boys from school and wrote in his own inimitable fashion, "Tiger didn't attend school because the horse fell in the well." While this was a perfectly honest note, neither the teacher reading that note nor any of the other students had wells or horses. So it was not surprising the excuse was dismissed and a new penalty imposed. It became increasingly apparent that we were misfit Billies in a rapidly changing world.

Bob's business brought him into contact with black people for the first time in his life. Prior to this, Bob, like many whites insulated by suburbia, blamed blacks for the ills of society. But Bob grew quite a bit from those early days. In fact, Bob came to trust and enjoy a certain black junkman named Frank Medley. Frank would come to Bob's shop and pick choice copper parts from his junk pile, like coils from alternators and starters. He would then weigh the copper, and offer Bob a fair price. But one day, Frank failed to come into the garage and settle with Bob. So the next time Frank came around, Bob approached him and said, "Frank, it seems you forgot to pay me last time around." Frank pondered slowly and said, "Shur nuf, Bob, shur nuf." They had a friendly relationship and Bob was on a *very* slow road to becoming a tolerant human being.

Bob ran for a local government office when we were kids. He put his hat in the ring for the position of Palos Township Road Commissioner. Of course he was imminently qualified because he repaired everyone's road construction machinery from miles around. But the incumbent was well known in his own right and held the position for 8 years at the time of this election. So name recognition came into the picture. The worst part for us, as children, was treating the children of this incumbent Commissioner well, because they rode the bus with us to school. And for a time, we actually felt like we should be at war with them. At the end of the day, Bob lost the election and we were left in an awkward position of facing those other kids as losers. How could their dad beat our dad? Impossible!

Bob contributed a few genetic peculiarities to his offspring. One of these was the *Morton toe*, so named to describe when a second toe is encountered that is longer than the big toe, and in more extreme cases, the second and third toes were found to be longer than the big toe. This made shoe buying particularly difficult as the kids always screamed shoes were too tight. That being the case, the Kuechers were a family of very large feet; most of the males sporting shoe sizes in the 12-14 range by their senior year in high school. Another peculiarity involved large hands and the fact that many of the children had longer ring fingers than index fingers. This configuration of digits is encountered most commonly in people of rage. No kidding. Yeah, a recent study surveyed hockey players most commonly in penalty boxes, people that serve time in prison etc. and came to this conclusion. And finally, there was the Kuecher nose, thickened at the bridge to participate in rough and tumble games but sometimes the bane of young girls trying to get noticed.

Bob's sister, Gladys, and her husband, Tom, were fairly heavy drinkers. Most photos of them were with drink in-hand. Gladys used to say "Buy some booze and forget your troubles." Gladys got sloshed one evening and told us, "There aren't any problems that can't be solved in the sack." Coming from a Catholic school, we probably did not fully understand the meaning of "in the sack" because of our nuns covert actions in scrambling such information.

Bob's mother, Grandma Kuecher, would come over once a week or so to cook wild game meals. There was a mixed blessing to her coming, however. On one hand, we loved the meals she would prepare. But on the other hand, there was an awful amount of hand labor required to accommodate her Old World cooking style. First off, one child had to retrieve from the freezer and clean between 6 and 10 birds; each bird requiring about 10 minutes prep work. Another child was responsible for washing and peeling a whole sack of potatoes. Two children typically had to man the potato grinder, one holding the base down while the other cranked the awkward grinder handle and pushed the peeled potatoes down the chute with a wooden block. And a child with very strong hands had to squeeze the potato grindings of their water content through a durable white sock or cheesecloth to make potato dumplings. All this was happening while another child would mix and knead the rye bread dough. At this point, Grandma may have seasoned the birds, lightly frying the pieces in garlic, and popped these into the oven in a gravy-like stew while dark German rye dough rose in a large bowl near the stove top with a clean cloth draped atop. This was all to prepare the main course.

Grandma also prepared wonderful desserts and she needed help with that task as well. She would send us out to pick rhubarb, clean it, chop it into 1 inch pieces, season with sugar and cinnamon and leave the pie filler in a bowl until the pie crusts were ready. That's not to mention the continuous stream of dishes that needed to be washed and floors that needed to be scrubbed and garbage that needed to be removed just to keep the operation moving forward.

Our cousin, Carol, remembers the girls starting the dishes after breakfast and finishing around lunchtime, only to start the process all over again for dinner. Let there be no mistake, it was always great to see Grandma. But considering the manpower required to get these meals to the table, it was also great to see Grandma leave. She wore us out!

One old world recipe Grandma Kuecher loved to make was turtle soup. Burlap sacks filled with nasty-tempered alligator snappers would be brought to the farmhouse and dumped on the driveway. The object was to offer the snapper a broom handle, let them lock onto it, pull the handle till the head was fully exposed and chop it off with an axe. Grandma's method for getting snapping turtles to push out their heads involved placing a hot iron on its back. Bob believes, to this day, that such a turtle's head, severed from its body, actually killed a chicken that pecked its mouth.

Another old world recipe from Grandma Kuecher's kitchen was corn meal mush. In it, corn meal was boiled until a thick consistency was achieved. Then the batter was placed in 4" by 9" loaf pans for cooling. Wax paper was typically placed atop each loaf to prevent condensation from wetting the loaf upon chilling in the refrigerator. In the morning, the loaf pans were inverted and thick slices were taken from the loaf. These slices were coated in crushed graham crackers and fried in butter on both sides. The end-product looked a bit like French toast left in the egg batter too long. On the fried corn meal we typically added more butter and this was topped with maple syrup, powdered sugar or jellies, in fact, whatever Babe had available.

The girls recall taking brief respites from Grandma's cooking in mid-afternoons. They recall Grandma and her worker bees sitting with a glass of tea and sampling the desserts while listening to Montovani or Burl Ives. And on occasion they would even partake in waltzing lessons in the kitchen, led of course by Grandma. Grandma Kuecher had a song in her heart.

41

Bob's mother, Grandma Kuecher in photo circa 1970.

Grandma Kuecher also loved gardening and planted some beautiful perennial flowers that bloomed each spring. On the southern side of the hill she planted peonies and irises, the former were white and pink while the latter were both the purple and yellow varieties. And on the top of the hill, Grandma planted a large plot of lilies of the field. These were beautifully fragrant little bells swaddled in over-sized, smooth dark green leaves. They were, and remain, a credit to their creator. But the most lasting gift Grandma left us was the rhubarb patch she planted near Bob's shop. Beginning in April, the kids would visit the patch on their walk home from school and look for evidence the rhubarb was sprouting. But it wasn't until May that the rhubarb was fully mature and ready for harvesting. Fully mature meant tall stalks that were red in color.

We were in tall cotton during rhubarb season. Rhubarb and strawberry rhubarb custard pies were just unbelievably delicious.

Grandma Kuecher suffered from angina and popped nitroglycerine tabs for as long as any of her grandchildren could remember. The children's knowledge of nitroglycerine, however, was limited to that gained from western movies, i.e. nitroglycerine was explosive. So needless to say we got a bit nervous when Grandma reached into her floppy purse for her handy little tabs. The prospect of an exploding grandma freaked the kids out and we gave her plenty of space.

Three of Bob's daughters later became involved in music and together with Bob started a variety band they called *The Family Affair* that played at weddings, picnics, parties and corporate functions. Bob let his instrument do the talking for him as he was quite shy in social situations. Bob and the girls dressed in formal attire for their engagements. In all, they played 10 years together and Bob remembers these as some of his best.

Music was very important to Babe and Bob. Virtually every evening, and especially on weekends, Bob would play his saxophone or his clarinet and listen to phonograph records of Montovani, Wayne King, and Chet Atkins. And Bob and Babe watched Lawrence Welk for so many years it seemed they knew the performers better than their own children. Like "haven't I seen you grow up?" Music calmed Bob's spirit.

Bob liked to barbecue for the family on his grill during the summer months. Bob had his own recipe for the burgers, i.e., thick with lots of garlic, egg, and Worcestershire sauce. He would cook the burgers fully but not till dry. They were always moist and tasty. Bob also liked to cook pre-soaked sweet corn on the husk and right on the grill. Babe would contribute a salad or beans. We ate together as a family at these outdoor barbecues. Bob, in this way, cared the family got together and did his part to see it happen.

Bob's mother, Grandma Kuecher died of a heart attack in 1974 and Bob's sister, Gladys, died of a stroke in 1976. This left Bob as the sole survivor of the family (in which) he was raised. And Bob, himself, had a heart attack when he was 54. No doubt, his risk for heart failure was complicated by smoking, stress, and a fatty diet as a young man. And he underwent quadruple bypass surgery at a time when this procedure was significantly higher risk than it is today. We visited him in the hospital on the eve of his operation and didn't know whether we would see him alive again. And there we stood, and there he lay. It was a bit awkward. He had always been so strong. But on this day, he shed a tear and we did also.

Bob recovered and did quite well, although it seems the family spent prodigious energies sparing this man from another heart attack. Today he walks daily. He retired from the everyday grind of the shop, and now takes anti-anxiety pills to 'take the edge off.' And he tries to be a new man around the house, one who cares about his family and listens.

Bob wrote a note to all the kids that included some core ideas he'd like all of the kids to embrace. His note was as follows:

Take the road less traveled
And let your imagination soar
Don't look to others to agree with you
They may be blinded by their own thinking

Bob continues to develop and test his ideas for changing the world. He jokingly says, "I suggest big oil companies either buy me out or suffer the consequences." You have to like his hubris.

Chapter Four

Babe and Bob's Kids

Babe and Bob had thirteen children in twenty years (1943-1963). Eight of these were boys (in fact the first four were boys), and 5 were girls. And because Babe had so many and so quickly, a burden was placed on the older children to assume responsibilities for the younger ones. Babe's children, therefore, took on roles consistent with their birth order. The older children were expected to be mature beyond their ages, the middle kids were expected to be somewhat responsible, and the younger kids basically had it made.

Babe and Bob were not the only persons in the family to sport nicknames. Their children were variously nicknamed Liza, Louie (a.k.a. Ever-ready), Farncis, Guppy, Nut (a.k.a. Queenie), Belle, Tiger (a.k.a. Nipsy), Tassy, Bass, Molock, Clarence (a.k.a. Turkey neck), Bird (a.k.a. Dodo), and Edweird. Then there were the workers and friends that came by our place with names like Tarbender (a.k.a. Black Bart), Jerky Burke, Slim, Hog Jaw, Hot Dogs, Homer, Jetox, Dog Face, Small Paul, Bunny, Herbie, Loner, Dago, Jackie, Hedda Mae, Bear, Shonitz, Higgs, Fitz, Pyts, Mott, Manual Labor, Schwer, One Eye, Sugar Bear, Nutsy, Crazy Dale, and Walking Jesus. Everybody had a nickname. Basically the nickname related a character trait or a story and that kept one in bondage to that association forever; perhaps not too differently from how Native Americans named their children. Tarbender, our first cousin on Bob's side of the family, was responsible for most of our nicknames. Questioning how one earned their nickname was answered best in the movie Animal House when an overweight, immature freshman asked the slob from the fraternity, "So why (did you name me)

Flounder?" To which the slob burped and answered "Why not?" If that logic causes you to shake your head, perhaps now you understand.

The first four boys in a photo circa 1948.

The oldest children were raised in a very rural setting. In fact, one of the older boys once walked the family dog to visit our neighbor, Anne Wilson, who lived about a half-mile away. Anne wasn't home so he opened the door of the chicken coop and both he and the dog entered. The dog then proceeded to kill every one of Anne's 23 chickens. Anne saw only feathers and an open door when she returned home. She declined Babe's attempts to reimburse her and gave up, thereafter, on raising chickens. That was life in the country.

Yet Babe and Bob's home on the hill was in the midst of transition from country to suburb, a change the family members resented and feared. In fact, our very address, 109th Street and 85th Avenue, gave us away as bumpkins. The number of times we had to explain why we didn't have an address like everyone else is incalculable. "Are you sure it isn't 10930 or 10950?" the pizza delivery man would ask. "No, we have no neighbors. We are the house on the hill" we would explain. "Oh" was his only response. "We'll leave the colored floodlights on so you can find us" we'd say. Sometimes you just felt like Jed Clampett.

We didn't have many neighbors and that was good. We had one neighbor about a half-mile to the SW, another about one quarter mile E, and a middle class subdivision about a half mile to the NE. Beyond these neighbors, there were seemingly endless corn and soybean fields. We had, as cowboy songs rail, wide open spaces. And because visitors were a rare commodity, our neighbors waited in great anticipation for us to knock on their doors for Halloween trick or treat. Were likely would be their only visitors. Looking back, there were only 900 people in the community in which we were raised and we knew everyone who belonged. Conversely we also knew who didn't belong.

This isolation produced a fear of outsiders. We were xenophobes. And collectively, we did our best to undermine efforts to develop the area around us, including the extraction of survey sticks as fast as they were placed. One posted sign entering the city of Palos Hills on Southwest Highway said it all, i.e., *Welcome to Palos Hills* and below a small sign added *No Trespassing*. We lived in that very diffuse perimeter where the city ended and the country began. And we viewed the city's encroachment like the native born Americans must have viewed manifest destiny. There seemed no way to stop it, but we were avowed to go down kicking.

Babe told a story about her eldest son that exemplified this *us against them* mentality. One day, a finely dressed man in a fancy black automobile pulled into the driveway atop the hill. The man identified himself as a US Marshall and asked to see the boy's parents. Her boy stepped up in defiance, however, and said, "If you were a US Marshall you would have a horse. Where's your horse?" Why is it that I hear *Dueling Banjos* whenever this story is told?

A farmhouse mindset continued in our childhood despite the fact the farm was no longer active. The kids raised turkeys and ducks, but the prospect of killing and eating these pets produced a ritual shower of tears, even if these animals proved unlovable or dumb as hell (like the white bunnies we would get on Easter that hid beneath the wheels of the cars and the cats that hid near the warm car radiator fans in the cold of winter).

Looking back, it appears that someone was always sick in the family and often these sicknesses swept the family like the plague. One reason, in retrospect, was the shortage of toothbrushes. Typically, there were only two or three toothbrushes in a cup or lying on the sink in our only bathroom. It was bad enough that the family shared its germs. But sadly, these toothbrushes were used for other purposes as well. In fact, one of the boys once scrubbed the stained porcelain sink with Drano (to remove the iron stains) and one of the younger kids came by a few minutes later and used this same brush for brushing her teeth. Her mouth bubbled and she screamed and ran for help. Such was the drama on our hill.

If children were home sick from school, Babe would typically tell them to go to her room and take a nap. But the children could not sleep in her room. Monsters emerged from the swirling wallpaper patterns so the kids would escape by opening the window, jumping to a nearby spruce tree, climbing down to ground level and running off free. Worse yet, Babe may decide to get this sickness over with and send you to see Hypodermic Sam, our burly family doctor. This man delighted in giving shots and of course we hated them. Seldom did we hear the sweet sound "I'll prescribe you some pills." Instead we heard," This shouldn't hurt. Relax and take a deep breath…" Ouch!!! A small consolation prize for enduring the shot was the Charm wild cherry sucker we received leaving the doctor's office. We were always damned glad to see Hypodermic Sam's office in our car's rear view mirror.

The children loved when the milkman came up the dusty road because of the delicious dairy chocolate milk he had on-board. The appearance of the truck prompted a classical Pavlovian response. Babe, typically, gave us specific instructions to purchase only white milk. But we saw our face-to face encounters with the milkman as an opportunity to not just have a good day but to have a great day. There was nothing quite like this cold dairy chocolate milk and we wanted it more often than not. Answering to Babe when we came into the house was sometimes awkward but seldom hostile. We would take what she dished out, drink our chocolate milk and get on with the day. We sometimes teased Babe when she crabbed at us. We remembered she at one time played the violin, so at times like these she earned the nickname, *'Fiddler Crab.'*

Babe and Bob's children experienced more than their share of accidents. The place we grew up was, in part, an industrial site due to Bob's business and accidents were potentially around every corner. Most of the accidents were of the sort nails in the feet, nails in the hand, cuts and bruises. But some of these accidents were more severe. For example, one of the older boys nearly had his foot cut off in a powered mower. This same boy was nearly killed in a tragic motorcycle accident, and our eldest boy broke his collar bone in a failed motorcycle jump.

The children all worked in Bob's shop in some fashion. If they were not involved in the repair business they were expected to remove the trash, sweep the floors, stoke the coal furnace in winters, or wash the tools in gasoline. We didn't use rubber gloves in those days and only God knows how much benzene and other carcinogens our skin absorbed. Fumes from engines were another environmental hazard to which we were exposed. And we played for hours with liquid mercury that Bob used in his testing instruments.

A landfill operation about a half-mile away posed new hazards. There is no telling how much damage the children incurred by playing there. Environmental consciousness had not yet arrived and we had no clue about PCBs and the like. In fact, one of the neighbors by the name of Hot Dogs found a pack of Twinkies at the dump and after a minute of Rodin-like consideration, opened the package and ate them.

Bob and his crew in the shop repaired the equipment of a number of heavy equipment operators and for the City of Palos Hills Public Works Department. It wasn't bad enough that legitimate repairs were made to failed equipment parts but there was also equipment damaged in good natured negligence. Case in point was the bearded, incredibly strong but sweet city employee that Tarbender called Walking Jesus. This fellow would tear off the stick shift on trucks as he roughly changed gears. He would then walk into the shop with stick shift in hand and Tarbender would sigh, "So what did you do now, Walking Jesus?"

Our family attended an ancient hilltop catholic church in Palos called Sacred Heart. The church was initially built in 1872 on Kean Avenue just north of 103rd Street. It accidentally burned in 1904 and was rebuilt the same year at a new site atop a hill just west of Kean Avenue on 107th Street. This new site, donated by a local black dirt farmer, provided a fabulous view of the glacial outwash-carved valley below and a popular sledding, tobogganing, and make-out area for the locals. We called it "the church hill." The church's Lenten service called "Stations Of the Cross" was really special. Mix that miraculous story, add some incense smoke, fling around some holy water and sing a few songs in Latin and you had all the ingredients.

The annual Church Picnic was a catered chicken dinner extravaganza with all the church members contributing in some way. The women contributed salads, desserts, and baked beans while the men typically manned the booths, parked the cars, set up the tables, planned and executed the games, and cleaned up the site after the event ended. And the Kuecher family band, The Family Affair, typically provided the musical entertainment.

The church's Holy Name Society met once a month in the church basement. There the boys would meet and hang out with the men from the community. Yeah, the meeting itself was boring and parliamentary, but that was a place where everyone knew you. Prayers before and after the meeting let you know this was foremost a house of the Lord. Cookie Claussen, Dickie and Charlie Busch, John Pospicil, John Ryan, Mr. Colclasure and the other elders were like family members to us and they kept track of us as the years went by. In addition, the Holy Name Society brought in guest speakers, sponsored a church softball team, hosted an annual White Sox game outing, and staged the monthly Bingo games held in the church basement. In short, the Holy Name Society was the engine of our local community.

Several of the older boys served as altar boys at Sacred Heart and on weekdays (they) were driven home by an impish old woman by the name of Gladys who could barely see over the dashboard in her black Mercury Comet. She was the most religious person they had ever met, voluntarily attending mass every day of the week. These same boys, as they grew older and learned to drive, sold newspapers at the church. And for this weekly service they earned between $4.00 and $5.00. That was a lot of work and a lot of hassle for a few bucks, especially since a few mornings were below zero Fahrenheit. Some may call such experiences character building, but it was more probably plain foolish. On balance, however, we did have some fun. We hunted during church services and many a time rocked the church with loud reports. And as the parishioners streamed out of church they would often ask if we got anything as they purchased their Sunday paper and dropped their monies into spent shotgun shell boxes.

Babe with six of her children
at her mother's bungalow in a photo circa 1962.

Catholic families, in those days, gave up meat every Friday, the idea being that if you missed the meat you would think of Christ. But in fact, we thought, "Christ, where's the meat?" Should one ever lose track of what day it was, you'd know for sure if tuna casseroles, fish sticks, or cheese sandwiches were being served. To complicate matters, Bob's generation truly felt they had not eaten if they were not served meat.

Babe, meanwhile, did not miss a beat and had children at a rate of one every 18 months in the course of 20 years. In fact, Babe was pregnant for 10 years of her life. But Babe loved her children and despite a well developed self-deprecating humor, she would, on rare occasion, bristle if outsiders or spouses bad mouthed her kids.

Babe enrolled the children at St. Michael Catholic Elementary school, about 10 miles SW of our home, in Orland Park. Our teachers, Dominican nuns from Boston, wore long, floor length white gowns, starched black and white habits, and a long rosary consisting of thick black beads and a heavy black wooden cross that dangled from a belt. It was not a smart idea to mess with the nuns.

The school's system of discipline was based on demerit cards. Five demerits meant you stayed after school. Ten demerits earned you two days after school, 15 meant you worked on a Saturday, 20 meant you worked two Saturdays and 25 got your butt expelled. Sister Eustace (also known as Sister Useless) let nothing pass. And on many occasions, we heard her siren call, "Kuechaah, bring me yaw caahd!" And we would watch her check one, two, three, four, five, (Good God, when does she plan to stop?), six, seven, etc. It was more than good fortune, however, that none of us got expelled. You see, our aunt (Bob's sister) cooked for the nuns and kicking a Kuecher out of school was not in her self-interest. And we made it to our graduations by the grace of God and a bit of politics.

Several of the boys served as altar boys at St. Michaels. This was our way to legitimately be dismissed from school. Father Coyle, a bald and distinguished priest, would take us out of school for funeral duty and we would be with him half the day or better in his fancy Lincoln Continental. Occasionally we got paid for this, but the biggest reward came every summer in our annual trip to Riverview, Chicago's legendary amusement park. Father Brogniac led the field trip. Prior to turning us all free in the park, he gave every boy $5.00

spending and a free admission pass. If you played your cards right and caught up with Father Brogniac later in the day, however, he was usually good for some additional cash. At Riverview it was always a test of bravery to ride the big, fast roller coasters, and with good reason. The clatter and clip clop of these coasters led one to believe each ride was an accident waiting to happen. So, in retrospect, it may not have been the heights or the g-forces, but rather the (lack of) engineering that scared the blazes out of us at Riverview.

As children, we were sheltered from the divisiveness of the world. We went to a catholic school and probably felt that all kids went to catholic schools. But as we matured we came to know there were two main groups of school age children in our little corner of the world, i.e. those that went to catholic schools and those that went to public schools. We referred to those attending the catholic school as *Catholics* and those attending public schools as *Publics*. That seemed to work for us, especially when our school played the public schools. We were fired up for these games. But we also realized we would be classmates and teammates a few short years away when we entered high school. Our world was further shaken to find many of our public school friends were also Catholics. In our simple minds we didn't think that was possible and it rocked our world.

The St. Michael school bus driver would treat the kids at the end of the school year to a Good Humor ice cream bar. This was such a treat to us. The vendor's white ice cream truck was parked at the intersection of Rt. 45 and 111th Street during the spring and summer months. The big decision we made as children was whether to choose the Toasted Almond or the Chocolate Eclair bar. The "Good Humor Man" would give you change from his coin sorter, lift the locking bar and open the freezer door. A whoosh of dry ice vapor was seen as he reached for the goods, an action that triggered Pavlovian tremors among the kids. OK, one could claim a bit of Irish bribery was involved here, i.e., good kids got ice cream. But it was also a kind gesture by a driver in a gentler, more compassionate time. He didn't have to do this.

Bob and Babe's children were born during the Cold War and fear of the Russians pervaded our lives. We practiced air raid drills in our schools and visited underground air raid shelters to practice our readiness. The Palos area, we were told, was a target for missile attack because Argonne National Laboratory's CP-2 atomic pile was built in the Palos Forest Preserves and a NIKE missile site was said to be located in nearby Orland Park. But by far the most terrifying message we ever heard on the loudspeakers at school was Walter Cronkite's announcement that President Kennedy was shot and pronounced dead. He was our charismatic leader and we knew not what life would be like after his passing. We were braced to go under the tables that day, and a few days thereafter, if air raid sirens were heard.

We, the children of Babe and Bob, were the generation of Hula Hoops, Slinkies, Tinker Toys, rubber faced stuffed animals, Pez candies, and yo-yos. We were the generation of Bob Dylan, Elvis, The Beatles, and Walter Cronkite. We were the generation of Popeil's kitchen inventions and muscle cars. And we were the disillusioned generation of Viet Nam. We were, in short, a generation that experienced profound change.

Black and white television became part of the family experience in the 1950's and early 1960's. The children watched *Buffalo Bob, TheThree Stooges, The Rifleman, Flash Gordon (who can ever forget Thun), The Lone Ranger, The Cisco Kid, Tarzan, Bishop Fulton Sheen, Tex Ritter, Lassy, Sky King, Sea Hunt, Clutch Cargo,* and *Mickey Mouse.* Aside from these programs, there were corny ads sponsored by Chesterton cigarettes, Hamms' beer, Burma Shave, Gillette razor, and the original Chicago discount car broker, Bill Moran. But perhaps the most interesting aspect of owning a black and white television in those days involved fixing it. The TV repairman had the coolest box of goodies the kids had ever seen. The box contained hundreds of vacuum tubes in tidy little boxes with nifty, numbered names. Surely one of these would do the trick. It was like magic!

The younger boys had mail duty. The family mail box was located about ¼ mile west of the house and it was our job, especially on weekends and during the summer months to pick up the mail for Babe. We'd walk down the dusty road and wait for the mailman to come. The mail box was our contact with the outside world. The boys reached out to the outside world through Charles Atlas paraphernalia, Estes rockets, and the submission of cereal box games (the stuff of higher level intellects).

The boys loved to play war games. In our war games, if someone shot you, there were two choices: you were wounded or you were dead. To mark ourselves as wounded, we used Babe's supply of sanitary napkins. We had no clue, I assure you. I don't remember if we used ketchup for the color effect or if we used the spent napkins. They looked like bandages to us. We must have been a sight.

In the 1950's and through the late 1960's, hunting and fishing were rooted parts of the local culture. We fished at many of the legal lakes in the Forest Preserve but one private mansion's pond off 131st Street was particularly memorable. It posted a sign "Beware of Dog." We would sneak into that property on summer evenings after midnight, take up our positions along the shore and hammer the bass and bluegills. The noise generated by all those strikes was certainly sufficient to alert the so-called guard dog but he must have been sleeping. That's all we could figure. And aside from the noise of the strikes was the noise generated by Jetox, a family friend that cried out, "Judas priest" every time he hooked a fish.

Hunting was a form of primal independence. Hunters, it was thought, were good providers. And those that returned home with *the goods* were to be appreciated as providers and warriors. Pursuant to this line of thinking was the desire to keep our rural paradise free of change, and free of the problems that plagued the outside world. The land would provide in the best and worst of times.

Pheasant hunting was a major fall event in our family and the boys were all quite involved. Typically one or two gunners were chosen to sit at the end of the field while the others drove through the field with dogs. Drivers got shots on birds that jumped close by and sitters had chances on birds that jumped ahead. And the sound of cracking corn stalks and swamp reeds was music to our ears as we pushed through the fields, guns carried chest-high and parallel to the ground.

During hunting season, the boys would walk down the roads with shotguns brazenly displayed and chat with police in passing squad cars. That was both a strange and beautiful partnership. They were happy for us. And hunting, at that time, was perfectly legal. Typically we would end a morning hunt with breakfast at the Grand Coffee Shop in Worth, Illinois. It must have been quite a scene for locals and city folk to see 4-6 big guys walk into the diner wearing camouflage and slide into the booths smearing feathers and fur on seat backs. Toto, this must be Kansas!

And because the boys and their friends loved their pheasant hunting, they went to some comical ends to preserve it. For example, Homer (one of our cousins) was once driving down our dusty road with his green VW Beetle and noticed a black cat in the weeds. Cats eat pheasants. So Homer grabbed a shotgun at our house, returned to the scene and kablang! When he returned to the hill he mentioned in passing that the cat looked a lot like his cat. And sure enough Homer's cat never returned home. Is there any doubt that the name Fruitcake Hill was well-deserved?

Back then, we were not so worried about posted signs. One brown, rectangular roadside sign was particularly amusing. The Forest Preserve District posted it and it read, "No hunting." Well that was just not true. There was great hunting in the Forest Preserves!

Goose hunting was another passion the boys shared. The paradox today is that geese are now everywhere people are, and not where they used to be, largely because people feed them. It's more typical today that upon returning home from an expensive goose hunt hundreds of miles away with a solitary kill, we'd encounter 100,000 of the creatures pooping in the nearby city park. If we had any sense we would stay home and hunt, or just go to the store and buy a goose.

One of the older boys got it in his head one evening to shoot a goose. He advised us he was on a mission and stated he must do it alone. So we butted out. He grabbed Bob's .22 caliber pistol, packed it in his gear and headed out into the cold winter night. About 4:00 AM, we heard a knock on the basement window and slid the window open. A large gray ghost flew through the air and fell with a splat on the floor. It was the biggest goose we had ever seen! "Where did you get him," we asked. "Little Red Schoolhouse" he answered. No, maybe we didn't hear that straight. So we thought we'd ask again and he confirmed our worst suspicion. He had killed the goose at a local nature center. How could you do that?" We really did not expect a straight answer because this was no more than a training exercise for this Marine. To this end, this brother was a family catalyst for risk taking. The rest of us wanted to seize the day but always had that guardian angel on our shoulder saying, "Are you crazy?" But like touching a hot flame and escaping unhurt, we somehow felt satisfied we took the chance. And we lived a risky, vicarious life through him.

As time went on, farmers began selling their fields to subdivision developments. Hunting was still legal but the new land owners were not nearly as obliging as our original neighbors. So we snuck into those properties at sundown, blazed away and got out. But the writing was on the wall that our hunting paradise was being systematically sold.

So we turned our attention to the Sanitary District because there was a great supply of birds that ate in the corn and soybean fields but nested in the cattail, Pampas grass, and thistle bottom lands of the Sanitary District. The Sanitary District, however, had a police force. We learned how to escape them by walking across the pipeline that crossed the Stony Creek. We got so good, in fact, that we could cross this 120 foot, 18" OD pipeline at a good walk. And the police could only yell (and gesture) as we escaped to the other side. We gestured signals in kind.

One day, in fact, an older brother and a younger sibling decided that Thanksgiving Day would be a great day to hunt some posted (no hunting allowed) lands in the Sanitary District. The logic was the police would be snoozing and off duty on Thanksgiving Day. Well after we shot a number of times the police showed up in force and our gamble they were off duty proved bust. We had police behind us, police on each side of us and police in front of us. And as we met the first squad car the middle son, talented in the art of negotiation, commenced his deliberations. The police, he realized really didn't want to punish them, only to teach them a lesson. And the parties had their say and all looked like it would end peacefully when the older boy, the Marine, leaned over to tell the younger brother that we should just tell them (the police) to get fucked. The younger boy smiled and hoped the police didn't hear but he said it again and loud enough that the police heard. And sure enough, we were off to the Palos Park police station on Thanksgiving afternoon. All in good fun! One of the boys carried a pheasant foot to class that he hid up his long sleeve shirt or sweater and when a question was asked the class, this boy raised his pheasant foot hand and the class erupted in laughter. The teachers never caught on. Pheasant feet also were great when you shook hands with someone. Ooh were they surprised! The texture was alarming yet people felt they should not look down as it would be embarrassing if it truly was a deformed hand.

Yackie was our hunting dog. She was a black and white Springer Spaniel with curly hair typically matted with stickers. To her canine mind, her sole purpose on earth was to hunt for us. She was a fabulous hunting dog and bounded high in the air when pheasants were near. We remember her nudging the bedroom door open at daybreak and laying her muzzle aside our faces. This was followed by a simple whine that escalated to hyper-ventilated bouncing, and then to barking. This dog was born to hunt. And on those days when we had to go to school, we would simply open the door and say, "Get em' Babe" and she was off to the hunt herself. But we remember most how happy she was to be appreciated. She would smile ear to ear.

When Yackie and our other dogs had puppies (there were numerous litters) it was cause for great celebration. We made a bed for the dog and puppies in the old stone basement just beneath the water softener and visited them regularly. Bob typically positioned a 100 watt light bulb nearby to keep the puppies warm on cold nights. And the kids would position each puppy to gain access to the mother's milk. It was such a joy to watch these animals with eyes frozen shut at birth develop their strength, open their eyes to the world, and learn to love us.

Each of the kids chose a puppy they liked best and immediately commenced a lobbying campaign to keep it. We typically kept one puppy from each litter. And we all remember the feelings we had when someone in the community would select the puppy we loved and walk out the door with it.

Then there was the legendary fighting rooster named Fred. Fred somehow took on a territory that included the house. There he'd be on the front steps making a stand to keep us out. He would flare his feathers and back up as you approached the front door. Then he would jump up and show his claws over and over. Bob kept a broom and the boys kept a hockey stick on the front porch to deal with Fred. We called him 'Rooster from hell.' He hated the boys. Surprisingly, a female cousin could hypnotize Fred by stroking his belly. We were all astonished. Many years later the author learned that DNA preserved in T-Rex bone marrow was found to be most closely related to chickens. That makes perfect sense, knowing Fred.

Bob and Babe's oldest girl owned a thick, strong, stubborn pony named Bubbles. He didn't like to be ridden, especially by the boys, and would commonly brush up to the fencing to knock off his riders. This didn't endear him to the boys, who used a rubber mallet to discipline him. Bubbles lived outside all year and grew a thick winter coat. One day, Bubbles got into a can of oats, broke his halter, and ran about a mile into a subdivision development. We found Bubbles at the end of a street grazing on green grass in a home's front lawn. When we arrived, a Doberman in that home was angrily hurling itself at the home's screen door. And in a flash, the door opened and the dog was down the stairs and nipping at Bubbles rear fetlocks like a boxer respecting the power of another man. Bubbles calmly continued to eat. But when the dog got within range, Bubbles cocked and kicked the dog end-over-end across the street. Wincing and hurt, the dog hobbled back into the house. Bubbles never broke stride and continued to eat, totally unfazed, as if to say, "Get outta here!"

On occasion, Bubbles would get into his can of oats and get super-charged with strength. He would then break his halter and run to the local tavern where he was a local celebrity. The patrons there considered him a good drinking mate. If the word delinquent applied to ponies, Bubbles would be the dictionary's exemplary case. Bubbles was also dressed each Christmas with deer antlers and marched to the front door where the older children introduced him to the younger kids as one of Santa's reindeer (that was) left behind.

And we shouldn't forget Stella the hamster in our all-star lineup of memorable pets. Stella was the pet of one of the younger girls. One day the boys noticed that Stella had been put on their elevated railroad board to keep her from running away. And so the idea developed that we could chase Stella around the track with the locomotive. Later we added a dart to the front of the locomotive and Stella really got moving. There was no malice or mistreatment because we really didn't stick Stella. It was more the fun of running the locomotive towards her and watching her reaction. This was done in good fun and we had lots of laughs, but we probably persecuted the child trying to protect the poor creature.

We purchased our guns and ammo from Nick's Gun Shop. Hot Dogs, one of the neighbor kids used to enter the gun store and say, "Say Nick, how's your dick?" And Nick would respond, "Fine! How's yours?" My wife, later in life, would say, "You really need to upgrade your friends." If she were around back then, we never would have been together.

Nick was not a very discriminate gun salesman. His assistant looked like a retarded pro wrestler. We called him Peahead. Nick sold us our conventional hunting supplies but went beyond. "Hey guys, (do you) wanna buy a cannon? "Yeah, sure Nick!" we would reply. Nick should have been more suspicious when we teenagers asked for black powder knowing full well we did not own a black powder gun. Instead, Nick would sell it *then* ask, "What are you guys going to blow up tonight?" And blow up things we did!

We detonated pipe bombs in a nearby sanitary landfill, generally under spent 55-gallon drums. These drums would launch vertically 100 or more feet into the air and on calm nights, strange mushroom-shaped clouds would sometimes hang over the dump, like Batman's signature. Babe and Bob were dining at a friend's home one evening when the largest bomb we ever made was detonated. Despite the fact they were inside and perhaps two miles from the site, they felt the rumble and called home to see if we were still alive. One of the boys used to say, "Make the news. Don't watch it." I guess we made the news. In retrospect we could have been blown to bits.

Turkey Shoots sponsored by the local Fire Department were annual events that our family greatly anticipated. There were two basic contests. The first was a target shoot in which 10 persons shot for closest to bull at a distance of about 70 feet. The second was an individual contest in which the contestant tried to tip a metal turkey head at 100 yards. The prizes for these contests were (you guessed it) turkeys. Frozen turkeys were the winnings-of-choice, but our family could only store three in our freezers. Family winnings in excess of three birds had to be taken as live birds. Thus you see how live turkeys became a yearly ritual in duty because we had to catch them each night to get them into their pens; and despair because the end of the road was always marked by their death, either by our hands or by foxes.

The boys, it seemed, were universally fascinated with power machines and should someone come over with a new Indian motorcycle or a hot car, the boys would stop what they were doing, perhaps light up a cigarette and take a slow walk around the machine, admiring it lustily. They would talk of muffler systems, carburetion, horsepower, and speed. And on occasion, they raced. Cousin Clem regularly raced for quarter mile times at the motor speedway. And other times they raced one another on 107th Street in the Forest Preserve. Mano y mano. They seldom spoke of close calls or accidents. My mother wouldn't want to know.

Nana, Babe's mother, stored her collectibles in a leather trunk in the attic of the old farmhouse. And like the story that Adam and Eve should not partake of the tree of good and evil, we children were told not to open or play with Nana's special things. After she died, however, the rules of the game changed and we opened the trunk. In it, we found over a hundred "78" albums of radio stars from the 20's, 30's and 40's. The boys didn't know what to do with these albums but we noticed they sailed beautifully. So we took them outside and with a few boxes of shotgun shells and enjoyed a memorable skeet shoot. Seventy-eights were brittle and thick and turned to powder (i.e. they *dusted*) when struck by shotgun pellets. Unfortunately, these records would be worth a small fortune today. How stupid could we be?

As youngsters, our only vacation (aside from the yearly fishing trip to Canada) was a once-a-year summer sojourn to that far away land of Joliet to the home of Babe's sister and our aunt, Mamie. Mamie's house was only 30 miles away as the crow would fly but it seemed like crossing the lower 48 to us kids. The roads were much slower then and we had to cross a dreaded swinging bridge en-route that scared us to death. We were told Great Uncle Joe Doyle drowned in that canal, and that made the canal crossing all the more dreary and those dirty waters the more foreboding.

Once we arrived in Joliet and received our room assignments, we went outside to play (and fight) with our cousins and their neighbors. The neighbor girl many years later reminded me we used to throw stones at one another *because* we liked each other. Rational minds cannot reconcile this behavior. Mamie recalls the boys going on bike hikes in her neighborhood with younger brothers in tow and returning, invariably, with no idea where the younger ones could be found. Perhaps the most amazing thing is that we survived at all.

Friends would come over on Friday and Saturday nights to play hockey. It wasn't regulation hockey, but street hockey played on the new addition's spacious basement floor. Sugar Bear, one of the family friends called the basement "The Cave". We played not with a puck but with a roll of electrical tape and our sticks were regulation and taped for battle. The rink's dimensions were uncertain game to game, depending on what Babe left on the floor and we didn't care to pick up. The key to scoring in our game of basement hockey was not necessarily beating the goalie with straight shots but to deflect the puck off the walls so the goalie didn't stand a chance. Babe got the short end of the stick when pucks were deflected and broke the basement windows. In these cases, we would duct tape a flattened box into the frame until the window could be fixed, and that sometimes meant enduring a few cold nights.

Another totally memorable experience was listening to our beloved Black Hawks hockey games in the Cave. Radio was the only way we could be with the action when the games were blacked out. We would turn the radio on and the lights off. And we'd listen to the great Lloyd Pettit describe the action in such visual terms that the game came alive. He could paint the picture like no one else. It was like you were there. But what I remember most is the angst of being *nearly the best* and hearing names like Beleveau, Richard, Mahovolich, Fergusun, and Sawchuck steal our dreams. We pained for Bobby Hull and Stan Mikita! Oh, how we pained! And that bastard Esposito, who was such an average player in Chicago, left the Black Hawks to become a super-star with our nemesis Boston. The Cave, no doubt, had its drawbacks. The basement was poorly ventilated and probably full of radioactive radon gas. And although we will never know the cause for sure, we lost one brother to pancreatic cancer in 2004.

A tradition at our house, with eight big boys in our family, was tackle football on Sunday afternoon. Our farmhouse was smack in the middle of hundreds of acres of manicured sod, the Warren's Turf Nursery. And all we had to do was drop shoes or shirts for the four corners and elect to receive or kick. Typically, friends came over as well and each side may have had seven or eight when all was said and done. This was rough play. There were some really big guys out there and they were doing some hitting. Weather conditions mattered not. If it rained, we played in the slop. And if it snowed we played in the snow. You could summarize the mentality here as *no excuses*. Unfortunately a fight between one of us and an outsider pretty well marked the end of our Sunday football games.

The boys also liked to play rubber ball against the wall. Younger brothers were at a distinct disadvantage, however, when they competed with their older brothers. You see, they had to lose. This was understood. So if a younger brother miraculously benefited from a lucky bounce or a lucky hit in baseball well the game just wasn't over. Or if it was, they played again, by God. This level of (un)sportsmanship was passed down the line. The middle child once approached his younger brother to apologize for treating him this way and he replied, "Hey don't worry, I did the same thing to the one below me!" One of my younger sisters once said, "Our family put the fun in dysfunctional."

A truly memorable and dysfunctional activity the boys and their friends enjoyed was taking a few cars to the Dog & Suds drive-in, parking along side one another, and flirting with the car hops. Occasionally, as the young maiden busied herself leaning into the windows of adjacent cars, one of us would "pull the grab" by pinching her on the bum. Needless to say, more than one serving tray was lost when we pulled the grab. And it probably was no surprise the same waitresses served us every time. In fact, they actually seemed to enjoy it, as we did. We'd probably be arrested for such behavior today.

Babe, typically, would get nervous if she knew the boys planned a drinking party at the house, so we seldom told her in advance. Instead we would tell her as the cars made their way down the dusty road. One of us would break the news to her in such a way she found palatable. For example we may tell her a few guys from the Holy Name softball team were coming over to have a few beers. That was mostly true. Babe was partially appeased knowing this was a Catholic activity and the guys were considerably above the legal drinking age. In actuality however the house filled with 50 and more, many of whom were below legal age. That didn't seem to matter too much when Babe was busy entertaining.

The weather event that best-tested our survival skill was known as *The Big Snow of January 26 and 27, 1967.* Over the course of two days, 28 inches of snow fell and the high winds that followed whipped the snow into drifts 5-6 feet high in places. The city was totally isolated but our family on the hill was in its element. We had wood to burn, heaters that could run on coal or gas, hand warmers, deerskin thermal gloves, thermal boots, a supply of food in the freezers, snow plows, and a survival spirit that wouldn't quit.

On the second day of the storm, Babe asked Bob to go to the

store for milk. The store was about a mile away and cars were useless so Bob said he would go in his grader. This grader was equipped with a massive v-shaped plow and a cab with a heater. One of the younger boys recalls going with Bob on this trip and how memorable it was to climb over giant drifts with this articulated machine. On the way home, Bob made a pass at busting through a particularly deep drift that crossed the road. He dropped the v-plow and hit the pile, making some progress but largely making a bigger pile. He backed up to get a second run at it and thump, an orange Volkswagen Beetle slid in the ditch. There were cars hidden in those drifts! Back home, the kids built spacious snow forts where the drifts were deepest, usually on the leeward side of wind-swept hilltops.

A few months after *The Big Snow* storm, a deadly tornado ripped through Palos. The tornado touched down on April 21, 1967 at 5:24 PM at 105th Street and Kean Avenue in a woody area locally known as Sullivan's Hill. The tornado moved to the northeast and cut a swath through a few family homes just north of 103rd Street and Roberts Road. Gaining strength and size across an undeveloped prairie, it emerged at the intersection of 95th Street and Southwest Highway in Oak Lawn, Illinois where all hell broke loose. Those present reported cars and buses going airborne, many landing on building roofs or atop other vehicles. The nearby Fairway Supermarket, Fisher's Motel, Suburban Bus and Suburban Gas station were completely destroyed and Oak Lawn High School suffered extensive damage. The tornado moved on to the northeast and died in Lake Michigan, covering 16 miles in 16 minutes, taking 32 lives and injuring 474. This storm became known as *The Oak Lawn Tornado.*

These weather events formed a centerpiece for local chronologies, i.e. people would relate to events by asking "Was that before or after the tornado?" "Before" "Oh, so it was after the Big Snow?" And so was born another Chicago communication stopper designed to confuse those not from the area.

Birthdays were the only day of the year you were honored apart from the rest. Needless to say, in a family of 15, the children rarely had special time alone with their mother. But on your birthday, Babe took you and you, alone, shopping. And later that day at the supper table, all the siblings sang and shared in one of Chicago's greatest treats, a Dressels Cake. The Dressels cake was made at a bakery in the City of Chicago's South Shore area at 1834 W. 79th Street. It was a layered chocolate cake with real whipped cream filling graced with chocolate shavings on the top and sides and a wonderful icing. These cakes were refrigerated and out-of- this-world delicious. The birthday child would get his or her preference for the location of their piece. Babe and her mother went out of their ways to order and pick up these cakes and they were memory makers. Other wonderful treats included homemade ice cream at the Plush Horse in Palos Park, "Rocket Sundaes" at Melody Lane, 1425 W. 87th Street in Chicago, or burgers and malts brought to you by Lionel trains at Snackville Junction, 109th and Western Avenue. Babe's teenagers, however, preferred the greasy sliders at White Castle on 95th Street. "I'll take a dozen with grilled onions." "And what will you have?" Nobody could figure if the patties in White Castle burgers were made of meat. Shonitz, a friend of the family, was convinced they were made of sawdust.

The two oldest girls reported more encounters with space aliens and UFO's than anybody in history. Perhaps the isolation of the hill facilitated such fantasies. They believed that we, at the farmhouse, were somehow chosen by extra-terrestrials to share an encounter. The obsession smacked of Spielberg's Devils Tower, with rays of light, the works. And the younger believes, to this day, that aliens came to her with lights and scared her. And she would cry at every movie and church service she attended. She claims her hyperbole is due to these unworldly encounters.

And while the first born girl got her warm fuzzies from being a good elementary and high school student, the second girl received the gift of cooking from Bob's side of the family. Her cherry pie was a finalist at the Illinois State Fair. The key ingredients included almond extract and real butter with fresh cream damped atop the crust. And she learned over time the power of her cooking in that she could make pies for teachers, bill collectors, whomever, and good things came her way. This bartering reinforced my suspicion that she was genetically linked to Bob's Bohemian lineage.

The two oldest girls in school photos circa 1960.

The seventh child, more specifically the seventh son in even larger Irish households, was earmarked by tradition to be the family's priest. This child did consider the vocation but it was not to be. There was just too much out there and he chose to be a scientist. He relayed a humorous story he heard somewhere that helped convict him he was doing the right thing. According to the story, a friar and his understudy were busy copying an old hand-written document when the understudy looked up at his aged mentor and asked, "Is it possible, teacher, that a single letter in a word was mis-copied and that the meaning now is totally different that what was intended, and that we have been reproducing that error for years?'

The old friar looked disturbed and said he would go in the basement and check. He came out a half hour later and looked to be shaken. "What's wrong?" the understudy cried. And the friar responded, "The word was *celebrate.*"

By the time Babe delivered her 12th child, she realized she could no longer carry the load herself. The job was just too great for one mother and she was overwhelmed. In fact, Babe made a few memorable telephone calls to Bob in the shop conceding the situation was out of control and asking for his back-up. In light of the home situation, Babe asked her mother, Nana, to care for this son in her Beverly home. Babe would deal with the rest of the family and visit him on the weekends.

So history repeated itself. Babe, herself, was farmed out to Julia in the country farmhouse and now one of Babe's children would be raised by her mother. So by the time this child was returned to the family at age 4, he was unfit for survival at the farm. His clothes were smart; he had no cuts or bruises, and had been treated like fine china. But he toughened up and became one of us, although his penchant for running the vacuum cleaner for hours on end did label him as a bit unusual.

For some unknown reason this child was terrified of a swirling pattern that played before each television episode of Checkmate. The boys thought they should break him of this fear and strapped him to a chair and placed him in front of the TV to face his demons. And he screamed! So that didn't work. He also loved Star Wars and Dr. Spock and he noticed that Spock's ears were not only pointed but they had some kind of plug in them. So this child figured he could be like Spock if he were to pack his ears with putty. Babe noticed it first. He didn't hear anything she said to him. Then she noticed the grout job he did on his ears and off to the doctor they went.

The two youngest boys started their own business on the hill. They called it the Shakey Shack. And the construction and accounting methods were, as the name suggests, shakey. It was nothing more than a piece of roofing that they propped up as a lean-to with a hole cut into the wall such that business could be conducted. Basically the biggest shareholder of this enterprise was Babe. If she had gone to the store and purchased fresh hamburger meat and other condiments, the Shakey Shack was open. No food in the house meant Shakey Shack would be closed. Babe's youngest child took the orders and served as cashier while his older brothers cooked the burgers and did maintenance. The Shakey Shack only had one repeating customer and that was cousin Tarbender. In retrospect, the Shakey Shack was a miserable financial failure. But we sure had fun. Maybe Shakey Shack was an early indicator of the children's business savvy. And perhaps this explains why our family did not produce entrepreneurial businessmen.

Babe's youngest child had a childhood speech problem and couldn't say his r's. A typical tutoring session with his brothers may go like this: "Say *crow.*" And he would say, "*cwoh.*" "OK, try *bastard*" and he would say "*bosstwahd.*" We loved hearing his personal touch on tongue-twister names in the Cubs organization like Beckert (bekwaaht) and Kissinger (kissinjwaah)! But our favorite was Ed's version of Packer QB, Bart Starr who he called Bwatt Stwaah. This same child woke Tiger on weekends for pancakes. He would stand by his bedside in his baby curls and diaper, dragging his blanket and exhorting him to wake. He called him Tigewa. This child tended to 13 ducklings we got somewhere and got the idea one day that these ducklings weren't getting enough to drink. So he got hold of each duckling and held its head under water for some time to assure it was no longer thirsty. And despite his stellar intentions, he killed every one of them.

Our cousin Timmy came to our house one summer and immediately took possession of the family tricycle. This caused a crisis among our own. Two of our younger boys, however, found a way to get Timmy off the tricycle by lighting firecrackers. After each report, they noticed Timmy got off the bike to check his tires.

Finally, in utter desperation, Timmy abandoned the tricycle and harmony returned to the hill.

Christmas was such a special time at the farmhouse. A 7-foot natural tree was placed squarely in the bay window such that its light could be seen inside and outside. And the anticipation grew with each passing holiday minute. Kids were out of school, the pressure was off, and it was great to relax and hang with the family. The fireplace was burning and if we were lucky, snow flurries drifted by the new addition's colored floodlights. On such an idyllic Christmas Eve, Babe and Bob arranged to have a large, jolly friend of the family dress up in a Santa suit and visit their youngest daughter. A buzz of activity acknowledged the arrival of the Santa entourage. The door was opened and Santa cried "Ho Ho Ho!" Santa waddled in slowly, then leaned down to say hello to this 4-year old and she exclaimed, "Hi Mr. Russo!" Busted!

Typically, the kids were told on Christmas Eve to go to bed a few hours after supper and advised that Santa would not come unless all the kids were asleep. Sometime around mid-morning the first kids would wake and the noise ramped up sufficiently to simulate a sustained nuclear reaction. The first thing the children saw as they approached the tree was the big ticket items like toboggans, sleds, and wagons. Next they would notice the sheer amount of gift-wrapped boxes. Consider, if you will, that each of the 13 kids would receive six gifts. That computes to 78 gifts not including the gifts for Mom, Dad, and Grandma! This mountain of gifts was then ferreted into individual piles with happy, toothless kids standing guard over their belongings. The first hour or so was unmitigated joy but as the night wore on, children's happy voices were supplanted by the endless drone of noise makers and Bob went to bed to cover his ears or just had another shot of whisky.

On one very special Christmas, Bob and Babe's third daughter organized a Christmas musical for our family that was especially memorable. It was a take-off from a Christmas puppet animation shown on Family Classics called Hardrock, Cocoa, and Joe. In it, she directed and played piano, while the children sang the parts of Santa's hard-working elves. A few select verses, provided from memory, went like this:

And Santa is busy with his heavy pack
He trusts his driver and never looks back
Oh di ole lady, Oh lady aye oh,
I'm Hardrock, I'm Cocoa, I'm Joe

It was such a cute play. And what brought the house down was the youngest boy's baritone rendition of *I'm Doe (Joe)*.

Scene from family play *"Hardrock. Cocoa, and Joe"* circa 1967.

The oldest boys, by this time were conscripted to the armed forces to fight in Viet Nam. That created some needed space for the rest of us, and bedrooms shifted about. But it also raised the anxiety of the family at large worrying about them day to day. Many of us wrote letters to these boys, if not daily then surely on a weekly basis. Dove-tailed with the boys' departures and returns were various new acquaintances and marriages. We were growing up and leaving the nest.

The farm house we were leaving was physically the same place of our childhoods, but it would never again feel the same. Time has a way of estranging us from our loves. And today we feel torn, i.e., we still love the people and the place but recognize it will never again be the same as it once was. Gone were the summer nights of chasing lightning bugs and placing them in bottles. Gone were the spring days of smelling Grandma's irises. Gone were the fall afternoons of raking leaves and throwing the football around.

The farmhouse today is in a state of siege. Subdivision homes now flank the property on three sides and a college is on the other. So it is a matter of time until the site is relinquished to development. Some call that progress. Our family would call it a damned shame.

Chapter Five

Reflections on the Farmhouse

No one could have foreseen the play set to motion by the union of Babe and Bob in 1943. They were a remarkable couple and they raised a remarkable family. Their children were proud to be Kuechers and all were above average in intelligence. In fact, nine of the thirteen children earned their Bachelors degree and three attained a Masters degree or better. That was progress over our parent's generation. And the four that did not finish their formal educations were successes in their own rights.

Babe raised us up to be Catholics and believed it was the only route to salvation. One has to respect Babe's conviction, whether founded or not, to deliver that message so passionately and so persistently. Kudos to Babe.

Having 13 children in today's age appears reckless, despite today's two wage-earner families. Tuition and medical have far outpaced inflation. But these concerns were not priorities in the social consciousness of Bob and Babe's generation. Children were a blessing. More children meant more blessings. And lower childhood survival rates required more children to offset these losses. Under these circumstances, parental attention was limited because it was just not possible to attend every basketball game and every activity of every child in a family of 13. So it appears as if we were reared and not raised. We've accepted this.

Bob and Babe in a photo circa 2000.

Bob and Babe's kids have applied the brakes on the population boom, however. One had 6 children, three had 4, and the rest were blessed with 3 or less. So in terms of size, Babe and Bob's family of 13 was special and probably will not be replicated any time in the near-future. But the bigger picture follows, i.e., how can 13 people living in the same house, with the same parents, eating the same food, hearing the same stories, and sleeping in the same rooms develop into adults that were so vastly different. But aside from the genetics with which we were born and the character building of our parents and friends, life's outcomes can be boiled down to a series of choices. Some of our choices are good while others are bad. But whatever choice we exercise, we live with both the rewards and the consequences of those choices.

Aristotle reportedly said, "You are what you repeatedly do." That being said, all of us were faced with challenges to change. And in the world in which we grew up, change was happening despite our objections. A Chinese Fortune cookie proverb said it best, "If you don't change the direction in which you are headed you will end up where you are going." Luckily, most of us changed our tacks.

Sunrise© greeting card illustrating life's irreversible choices.

Babe and Bob believed in the American entrepreneurial spirit and believed there were no gains without risk. Pursuant to this strategy, Babe and Bob invested considerable amounts of money into two family businesses. Perhaps they should have folded their cards and walked, but they didn't. That was their choice, among many others.

To this day, Babe and Bob's children communicate with each other largely by calling Babe and asking Babe to relay their message. Of course that's unfair to Babe. But Babe plays along because it gives her a reason to call one of the children she has not called in some time. The losers in this arrangement are the children. In fact, families that drop off Christmas presents for each other at Babe's have discovered that some years they received two presents because Babe never got around to delivering the first.

Bob and Babe in photo circa 2004.

Visiting the farmhouse today you will be greeted by a chorus of barking dogs. Barking is how the dogs earn their keep. The visitors should not lose focus on their first task, however, and that is to negotiate the yard's minefield of boopies. Once inside, you will be greeted by the dogs and see Bob in his leather chair at the far end of the family room. Babe will greet you at the door shortly thereafter, apologizing for the way her hair looks, the condition of the house, or both.

The farmhouse today is in jeopardy of being swallowed by the city. Bob and Babe's plan is to stay on the property as long as they are physically and fiscally capable of doing so. The farmhouse, 137 years old and counting, is one of the oldest remaining structures in Cook County and the property on which it stands has been continuously owned by descendants of Richard O'Connell for 155 years and counting. But fixing it to reside in it is another story. The cost of repair would clearly exceed the value of the old structure. So we appear to be looking at a relic of the past and not a vision of the future. This is a sad realization after all the living that has gone on in this structure by a single family.

Despite its physical condition, the farmhouse remains the center of our family universe. It is like the hub of a wheel. Some view this favorably, suggesting the farmhouse provides a rock on which we anchor our unsteady lives. Others claim the farmhouse tethers families and is insensitive to the doings of families spinning about it. Both claims are probably true.

The satellite image that follows reveals the encroachment of the city and the college on the rural life we knew as children. The hill is designated by the property inside the white dash while peat swamps and tall grass prairie encircled the hill. The farmhouse is located at the point of the arrow. Other structures atop the hill include Bob's garages and various rental properties. Moraine Valley Community College properties surround the family's acreage position.

Over the years, the family has suffered emotional loss because we recognize things on the hill will never be the way they once were. Our family experienced loss because we valued our childhood. Reality screams it's over now and we must move on. But it's a bit like severing the umbilical to a world we preferred.

Bob and Babe's children pine tirelessly over trivia of our childhood. One of the siblings may remember our first phone number, Gibson 8-4158. Another may remember our shoe salesman, Dave Hurwitch, our dentist Dr. Randall, or our church organist, Mrs. Grimes. And another may remember the way the kids would sneak into the unheated back porch and snack on the leftover turkey, cranberries, and pies. Our lives are a collection of such memories. These memories form a tapestry that reminds us how blessed we were to have shared this hilltop experience with so many. It was a unique time and place and we were fortunate to have been along for the ride. It was a time for us.

So here we sit in the present, too late to turn back and too scared to venture an alternative. It's apparently more comfortable to keep bumbling along doing what we are doing. That way time passes. And isn't that ultimately our goal, i.e. to pass the time and do it in some comfort? Then we can all pine one day that life has passed us by. Such floods of thought are the rainfall of who we once were.

The stories presented in this memoir are excerpts from our lives as children but do not represent the total experience of life on the hill. In fairness, there were interludes of grave normalcy where Babe's management skills carried the family flawlessly and difficulties went largely un-noticed. Bob and Babe were always in the background during these times quietly sculpting our lives and for this we can all say Thank You for a job well done!

Newsweek columnist Anna Quindlen commented recently about raising her own children, and I think this is appropriate to Bob and Babe's uncertainties in raising their lot. She said, "Raising children is presented at first (to young parents) as a true-false test, then it becomes multiple choice, and further along you realize it was an endless essay where nobody knew anything for sure." Bob and Babe, like Ms. Quindlen, learned to trust themselves in parenting. Bertram Russell resounded on the theme saying, "The central problem in our day is acting decisively in the absence of certainty." Babe and Bob somehow found their way. It wasn't easy.

In retrospect, the common link between the farmhouse inhabitants, past and present is our Irish heritage. Babe's sister, Mamie, exhorted all her children, nephews, and nieces to visit

Ireland and come full circle on their heritage. And perhaps in time our Irish-American heritage, and not the hill, will emerge as our enduring anchor. That is a more portable and enduring legacy.

About the Author

Gerald Kuecher was born in 1951, the seventh child of Bob and Babe Kuecher's 13 children. All the kids knew him as Tiger. In fact, when people would call the house and ask to talk to Gerald, his brothers and sisters would respond, "I'm sorry. No Gerald lives here. You must have the wrong number!"

This strawberry blonde was battle-tested from warring all those years with his big athletic brothers and on one occasion. an elderly Bostonian nun approached to smack him for chewing gum during her class but withdrew saying, "Kuechaah, I'd hit you but yaw so hahd ah might hurt mah haynd!" In a distinct duality, however, Tiger had a compassionate heart and cried at strangers funerals as an altar boy. These character traits of competitiveness and compassion marked his life.

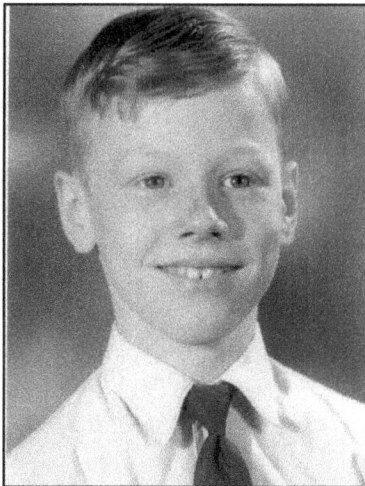

Gerald Kuecher in school photo circa 1962.

As a teenager, Gerald became interested in the physical sciences after reading reports by the Illinois Geological Survey concerning the glacial history of the Palos area. He went on to earn a Ph.D. in Geology and has published numerous technical articles. This book is his first venture into non-technical literature. He lives presently in Dhahran, Saudi Arabia but has maintained a home in Houston, Texas.

Gerald Kuecher in a photo circa 2003.